DATE DUE

Interesting Athletes

*Dedicated to
my late wife, Jennie
my son, Richard
my granddaughter, Terri
my late brother, Bill
and my great-granddaughter, Corryn*

Interesting Athletes

A Newspaper Artist's Look at Blacks in Sports

by
George L. Lee

McFarland & Company, Inc., Publishers
Jefferson, North Carolina, and London

On the title page: self-portrait by the author

British Library Cataloguing-in-Publication data are available

Library of Congress Cataloguing-in-Publication Data

Lee, George L., 1906–
    Interesting athletes : a newspaper artist's look at Blacks in
sports / by George L. Lee
        p. cm.
    [Includes index.]
    ISBN 0-89950-482-5 (sewn softcover; 50# acid-free natural paper) ∞
    1. Afro-American athletes—Biography.   2. Athletes, Black—
Biography.   3. Afro-American athletes—Portraits.   4. Athletes,
Black—Portraits.   5. Pen drawing.   I. Title.
GV697.A1L37   1990
796'.092'2—dc20   89-29306
[B]   CIP

Printed in the United States of America

McFarland & Company, Inc., Publishers
    Box 611, Jefferson, North Carolina 28640

Contents

Note: Players can appear on more than one page or in more than one section.

Preface

I arrived in Chicago in September of 1927, right after the Gene Tunney–Jack Dempsey second title fight. On September 23, 1926, Tunney had won the world's heavyweight title from Dempsey. In the second fight, on September 22, 1927, Tunney retained his title.

I was full of high hopes and perhaps a bit apprehensive in a new world. I was seeking a Negro newspaper that would use my sports drawings. I was 21 with ambition but no experience.

In 1929 my first misadventure was starting a neighborhood newspaper with a friend. I guess I was looking for a spot for my drawing. Neither one of us had any money or experience, but we started the *South-Center Advertiser* with the idea of selling enough advertising to make it. It was a giveaway paper. We soon realized our mistake—and you remember what happened in the fall of 1929 . . . THE BIG STOCK MARKET CRASH.

I contacted a boxing magazine named *Bang*. It was, finally, what I had been looking for—a chance to make sports drawings. *Bang* was sold at the Chicago Stadium and I soon made contacts with the publishers. So in my spare time I was busy drawing.

In 1930 I met Eddie Geiger, sports editor of the *Chicago American,* an evening Hearst paper. Sports cartooning was a big thing and it was very exciting to me. My work first appeared in the *American* when Eddie let me make a drawing of Herman Brix, a British shot-putter (United States track meet at Soldier Field on August 26, 1930). I was hired on a freelance basis.

I was looking for an opportunity and I was mighty proud and happy. Henry M. Dawes, president of the Pure Oil Co., and a brother of U.S. Vice President Charles G. Dawes, wrote me a letter of congratulations for my drawing in the *American*. It led to drawings of the company executives for the cover of the *Pure Oil News,* the company magazine.

I still had a commercial art school on my mind so I went to the Vogue Art School and I was politely told that they didn't accept Negro students. So I enrolled at the Art Institute. I didn't like figure drawing and I gave up on art study and decided I would stick to the newspapers.

Preface

Eddie Geiger liked my sports drawings. I tried to get a job doing anything to be able to draw but with no luck. I kept grabbing at anything he would let me do . . . billiard matches, six-day bike races, wrestling, boxing and baseball. The morning William Wrigley, the Chicago Cubs owner and chewing gum magnate, died. Eddie used a drawing that I had made for an early edition.

Lucius Harper, managing editor of the *Chicago Defender*, got in touch with me and asked me to draw a weekly sports cartoon. In January of 1934 I started a weekly "Sporting Around" series. I had come to his attention by my drawings in the *American*.

In 1934 Joe Louis was being hailed as the world's greatest amateur boxer in the light-heavyweight class. I was in George Trafton's office in his gym on Randolph Street when he received a wire saying that Joe was going to turn pro. Trafton, an ex–Bears lineman, promoted Joe's first fight at Bacon's Casino, outdoors at 49th and Wabash. The fight was held on July 4, 1934, and Joe's first opponent was Jack Kracken. Joe knocked him out in the first round. Joe received $50 for his first pro fight and I drew ten posters advertising the fight for which I received $50. Joe Louis was a great champion – the first black since Jack Johnson had won the title from Tommy Burns at Sydney, Australia, on December 26, 1908. (I had the pleasure of being in the company of Johnson once in the city room of the *Defender*.)

In the fifties, the International Boxing Club was formed with James Norris as president and Truman Gibson, Jr., as secretary. Izzy Kline, a trainer whom I had known during earlier Chicago Stadium days, was connected with the group. I went to see him about drawing boxing cartoons and I was readily accepted. All during the fifties I was kept busy drawing publicity and sports cartoons, which were published in the *Chicago Tribune* and the *Chicago Defender*.

With television, interest in boxing became even more widespread. By this time Joe Louis was nearing the end of his career but it was a period of great fights and champions. The government began to investigate the International Boxing Club and claimed they had a monopoly on boxing. The government won and in 1959 the International Boxing Club disbanded.

Interesting Athletes represents the highlights of my career in drawing sports. The greatest thing one can have is TIME. To be able to live long enough to strive to accomplish something is a privilege. I hope this collection of my sports drawings gives enjoyment to all sports fans.

Because I was living and working in Chicago, many of the athletes depicted in this book are those whose career brought them to the Chicago area. Since boxing was a major sport in Chicago, boxing is well represented in the pages of this book. However, because much of my work appeared in

Preface

publications that were interested in publicizing the achievements of all blacks, there were opportunities to depict black athletes involved in many types of sports.

The pages in this book are the footprints in the sand of my sports career as a self-made cartoonist. These drawings did not seem so important at the time they were drawn but as present and future generations look back at the athletes depicted it seems natural that we would want to preserve for them these unique documentations of achievement and glory. All drawings were once published.

With enthusiasm and great pride, using a sheet of coquille board, a Korns Lithograph pencil, a pen and a bottle of India ink, I strived to bring the athletes to life. I will always be grateful to have been a part of the now mostly lost world of the Sports Artist.

George L. Lee
Chicago
Fall 1989

Boxers—
American
and World

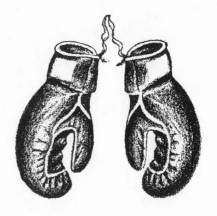

THE BLACK TERROR

BILL RICHMOND
1763 - 1829

FIRST AMERICAN BLACK TO GAIN BOXING FAME IN ENGLAND. BORN OF SLAVE PARENTS IN CUCKHOLD, STATEN ISLAND, NEW YORK, LATER KNOWN AS RICHMOND, S.I. DURING THE WAR OF INDEPENDENCE HIS MASTER FLED TO ENGLAND, LEAVING HIS SLAVES. THE DUKE OF NORTHUMBERLAND THE HEAD OF THE BRITISH ARMY ON STATEN ISLAND TOOK A FANCY TO THE BOY AND MADE HIM HIS VALET AND TOOK HIM TO ENGLAND. THE DUKE SENT HIM TO SCHOOL. A SCHOLARLY BOY HE LEARNED CABINET-MAKING. OFTEN INSULTED HE WAS CAPABLE OF DEFENDING HIMSELF SO WELL THAT HE WAS ENCOURAGED TO TAKE UP BOXING

Geo Lee

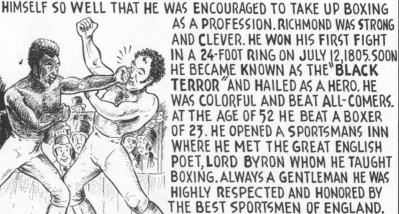

AS A PROFESSION. RICHMOND WAS STRONG AND CLEVER. HE WON HIS FIRST FIGHT IN A 24-FOOT RING ON JULY 12, 1805. SOON HE BECAME KNOWN AS THE "BLACK TERROR" AND HAILED AS A HERO. HE WAS COLORFUL AND BEAT ALL-COMERS. AT THE AGE OF 52 HE BEAT A BOXER OF 23. HE OPENED A SPORTSMANS INN WHERE HE MET THE GREAT ENGLISH POET, LORD BYRON WHOM HE TAUGHT BOXING. ALWAYS A GENTLEMAN HE WAS HIGHLY RESPECTED AND HONORED BY THE BEST SPORTSMEN OF ENGLAND.

FIRST AMERICAN BOXING CHAMPION

TOM MOLINEAUX
1784 - 1818

BORN INTO THE **SLAVE** FAMILY OF **SQUIRE MOLINEAUX**, IN RICHMOND, **VA**. **BARE KNUCKLE** FIGHTING STARTED IN **ENGLAND** IN 1716. NOT **UNTIL 1810** DID **AMERICA** MAKE A **DEFINITE BID**, WHEN **MOLINEAUX** WENT TO **ENGLAND** TO **FIGHT TOM CRIBB** THE **ENGLISH CHAMPION**. THEY MET ON DEC 18. IN THE **31ST** ROUND **TOM** FLOORED **CRIBB** - BUT IN DOING SO, HE **FELL** BACKWARDS **STRIKING** HIS **HEAD**. DAZED, THE FIGHT ENDED IN THE **33RD** - **CRIBB** THE WINNER.

YE GAD WHATTA MAN!

BY JOVE

Geo Lee

JACK L. COOPER
1889 - 1970

FIRST **BLACK RADIO** PERSONALITY IN THE **NATION** WAS BORN IN MEMPHIS, TENN. ONCE A **VAUDEVILLE** TROUPER, A **LIGHTWEIGHT** BOXER AND A **NEWSPAPERMAN**. STARTED HIS RADIO CAREER IN 1924 WITH **STATION WCAP** IN WASH, D.C. IN 1928 HE AIRED HIS **FIRST** CHICAGO PROGRAM. HE **STAYED** ON THE AIR UNTIL 1961.

WSBC

3

THE BLACK PRINCE

PETER JACKSON
1861 - 1901

PERHAPS THE GREATEST HEAVY-WEIGHT FIGHTER OF HIS DAY. BORN IN THE VILLAGE OF FREDERIKSTED IN ST. CROIX, VIRGIN ISLANDS. HIS FAMILY MOVED TO AUSTRALIA WHEN HE WAS 6. HE BECAME A BOATMAN AT 14. A SAILOR AT 16. A POWERFUL LAD HE WAS AN EXCEPTIONAL SWIMMER AND DIVER. HIS COURAGEOUS EXPLOITS OF SWIMMING IN DANGEROUS SEAS INFESTED WITH MAN-EATING SHARKS AND THE DREADED OCTOPUS WERE WELL KNOWN. HE STARTED HIS BOXING CAREER IN 1882 AND ON SEPT 25, 1886 WON THE AUSTRALIAN CHAMPIONSHIP FROM TOM LEEDS IN THE 30th Rd. IN 1888 HE WENT TO AMERICA AND SAN FRANCISCO. JOHN L. SULLIVAN, THE WORLD CHAMPION DREW THE COLOR-LINE AND REFUSED TO FIGHT HIM. JACKSON NEVER WON THE WORLD TITLE...BUT BEAT THE BEST OF THE OTHERS. HIS MOST FAMOUS FIGHT WAS A 61-Rd DRAW WITH GENTLEMAN JAMES J. CORBETT IN 1891. HE KO'D PADDY SLAVIN FOR THE BRITISH EMPIRE TITLE IN LONDON IN 1892. HIS HEALTH FAILING HE LOST TO JIM JEFFRIES IN 1898. THE BLACK PRINCE'S CAREER ENDED IN 1899. HE ENTERED BOXING'S HALL OF FAME!

Geo Lee

© 1974 George L. Lee Feature Service

4

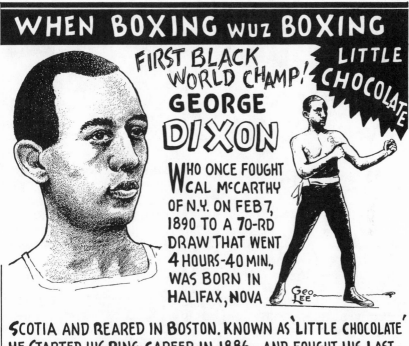

WHEN BOXING wuz BOXING

FIRST BLACK WORLD CHAMP! **LITTLE CHOCOLATE**

GEORGE DIXON

WHO ONCE FOUGHT CAL McCARTHY OF N.Y. ON FEB 7, 1890 TO A 70-RD DRAW THAT WENT 4 HOURS-40 MIN., WAS BORN IN HALIFAX, NOVA

SCOTIA AND REARED IN BOSTON. KNOWN AS 'LITTLE CHOCOLATE' HE STARTED HIS RING CAREER IN 1886...AND FOUGHT HIS LAST FIGHT IN 1906...20-YEARS IN THE RING. ONE OF THE GREATEST LITTLE BOXERS OF ALL TIME. DIXON WON THE WORLD BANTAM WEIGHT TITLE (112 lbs) WHEN HE KO'D NUNC WALLACE OF ENGLAND IN LONDON ON JUN 27, 1890. HE WON THE WORLD'S FEATHER-

WON AND LOST THE FEATHER-WEIGHT CROWN 4-TIMES

WEIGHT CHAMPIONSHIP WHEN HE KO'D CAL McCARTHY OF JERSEY CITY, IN THE 22nd RD AT TROY, N.Y. ON MAR 31, 1891. DIXON NEVER WEIGHED OVER 118 lbs!

I'M TIRED — ME TOO

...AFTER 70-ROUNDS OF FIGHTIN' IT WAS A DRAW!

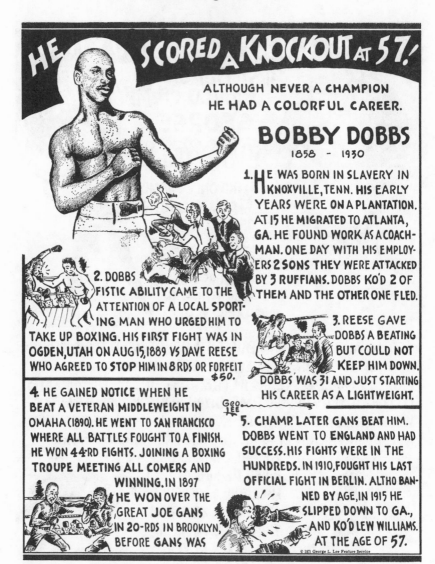

HE SCORED A KNOCKOUT AT 57!

ALTHOUGH NEVER A CHAMPION
HE HAD A COLORFUL CAREER.

BOBBY DOBBS
1858 - 1930

1. HE WAS BORN IN SLAVERY IN KNOXVILLE, TENN. HIS EARLY YEARS WERE ON A PLANTATION. AT 15 HE MIGRATED TO ATLANTA, GA. HE FOUND WORK AS A COACHMAN. ONE DAY WITH HIS EMPLOYERS 2 SONS THEY WERE ATTACKED BY 3 RUFFIANS. DOBBS KO'D 2 OF THEM AND THE OTHER ONE FLED.

2. DOBBS FISTIC ABILITY CAME TO THE ATTENTION OF A LOCAL SPORTING MAN WHO URGED HIM TO TAKE UP BOXING. HIS FIRST FIGHT WAS IN OGDEN, UTAH ON AUG 15, 1889 VS DAVE REESE WHO AGREED TO STOP HIM IN 8 RDS OR FORFEIT $50.

3. REESE GAVE DOBBS A BEATING BUT COULD NOT KEEP HIM DOWN. DOBBS WAS 31 AND JUST STARTING HIS CAREER AS A LIGHTWEIGHT.

4. HE GAINED NOTICE WHEN HE BEAT A VETERAN MIDDLEWEIGHT IN OMAHA (1890). HE WENT TO SAN FRANCISCO WHERE ALL BATTLES FOUGHT TO A FINISH. HE WON 44 RD FIGHTS. JOINING A BOXING TROUPE MEETING ALL COMERS AND WINNING. IN 1897 HE WON OVER THE GREAT JOE GANS IN 20-RDS IN BROOKLYN, BEFORE GANS WAS

5. CHAMP. LATER GANS BEAT HIM. DOBBS WENT TO ENGLAND AND HAD SUCCESS. HIS FIGHTS WERE IN THE HUNDREDS. IN 1910, FOUGHT HIS LAST OFFICIAL FIGHT IN BERLIN. ALTHO BANNED BY AGE, IN 1915 HE SLIPPED DOWN TO GA., AND KO'D LEW WILLIAMS. AT THE AGE OF 57.

SAM LANGFORD
1886 - 1956

ONE OF AMERICA'S GREATEST FIGHTERS OF ALL-TIME, WAS BORN IN WEYMOUTH, NOVA SCOTIA. HE RAN AWAY FROM HOME AND WENT TO BOSTON, MASS., WHERE HE BEGAN A CAREER OF BOXING THAT LASTED FROM 1902 TO 1923. HE WAS CREDITED WITH 642 BOUTS BUT FATE KEPT HIM FROM BEING A WORLD CHAMPION. HIS ABILITY WAS UNDISPUTED. SAM WAS 5'6½"

AND DESPITE HIS TOP WEIGHT OF 162 HE FOUGHT HEAVYWEIGHTS. HE BEAT THE OLD MASTER-LIGHTWEIGHT CHAMP JOE GANS IN 15-RDS BUT THE TITLE WAS NOT AT STAKE. FOUGHT A DRAW WITH JOE WALCOTT THE WELTERWEIGHT CHAMP. MIDDLE-WEIGHTS SOON AVOIDED HIM AND HE HAD TO FIGHT HEAVIES. HIS MOST MEMORABLE FIGHT WAS A 15-RD LOSS TO JACK JOHNSON WHO OUT-WEIGHED HIM BY 49 POUNDS (1906). AFTER HIS LONG CAREER HE BECAME BLIND, IN 1924. HE DIED PENNILESS IN CAMBRIDGE, 3-MONTHS AFTER HE GAINED **HALL** OF **FAME** RECOGNITION.

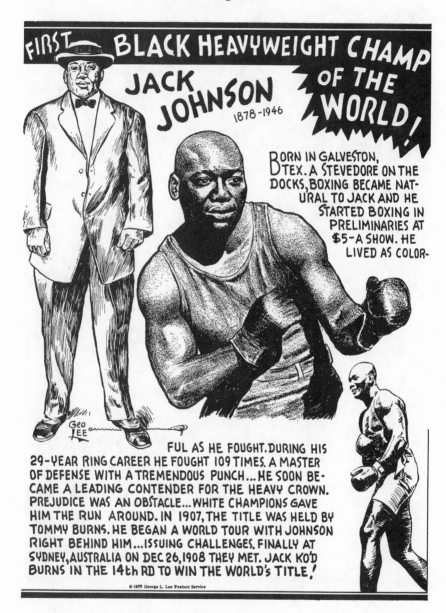

FIRST BLACK HEAVYWEIGHT CHAMP OF THE WORLD!

JACK JOHNSON 1878-1946

BORN IN GALVESTON, TEX. A STEVEDORE ON THE DOCKS, BOXING BECAME NATURAL TO JACK AND HE STARTED BOXING IN PRELIMINARIES AT $5-A SHOW. HE LIVED AS COLOR-

FUL AS HE FOUGHT. DURING HIS 29-YEAR RING CAREER HE FOUGHT 109 TIMES. A MASTER OF DEFENSE WITH A TREMENDOUS PUNCH... HE SOON BECAME A LEADING CONTENDER FOR THE HEAVY CROWN. PREJUDICE WAS AN OBSTACLE... WHITE CHAMPIONS GAVE HIM THE RUN AROUND. IN 1907, THE TITLE WAS HELD BY TOMMY BURNS. HE BEGAN A WORLD TOUR WITH JOHNSON RIGHT BEHIND HIM... ISSUING CHALLENGES. FINALLY AT SYDNEY, AUSTRALIA ON DEC 26, 1908 THEY MET. JACK KO'D BURNS IN THE 14th RD TO WIN THE WORLD'S TITLE!

© 1975 George L. Lee Feature Service

Chicago Defender   December 21, 1935

KID CHOCOLATE

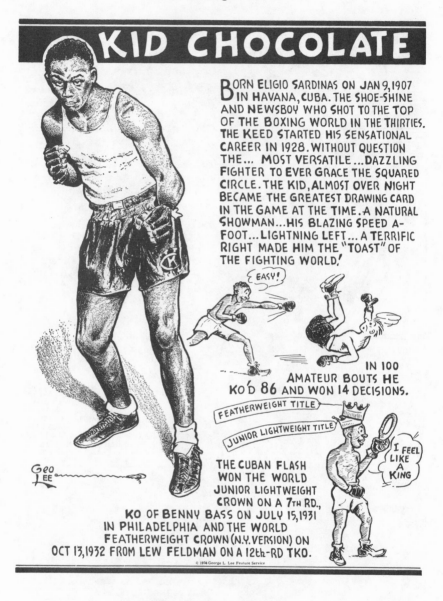

BORN ELIGIO SARDINAS ON JAN 9, 1907 IN HAVANA, CUBA. THE SHOE-SHINE AND NEWSBOY WHO SHOT TO THE TOP OF THE BOXING WORLD IN THE THIRTIES. THE KEED STARTED HIS SENSATIONAL CAREER IN 1928. WITHOUT QUESTION THE... MOST VERSATILE...DAZZLING FIGHTER TO EVER GRACE THE SQUARED CIRCLE. THE KID, ALMOST OVER NIGHT BECAME THE GREATEST DRAWING CARD IN THE GAME AT THE TIME. A NATURAL SHOWMAN...HIS BLAZING SPEED A-FOOT...LIGHTNING LEFT... A TERRIFIC RIGHT MADE HIM THE "TOAST" OF THE FIGHTING WORLD.'

EASY!

IN 100 AMATEUR BOUTS HE KO'D 86 AND WON 14 DECISIONS.

FEATHERWEIGHT TITLE

JUNIOR LIGHTWEIGHT TITLE

I FEEL LIKE A KING

THE CUBAN FLASH WON THE WORLD JUNIOR LIGHTWEIGHT CROWN ON A 7TH RD., KO OF BENNY BASS ON JULY 15, 1931 IN PHILADELPHIA AND THE WORLD FEATHERWEIGHT CROWN (N.Y. VERSION) ON OCT 13, 1932 FROM LEW FELDMAN ON A 12th-RD TKO.

Geo Lee

10

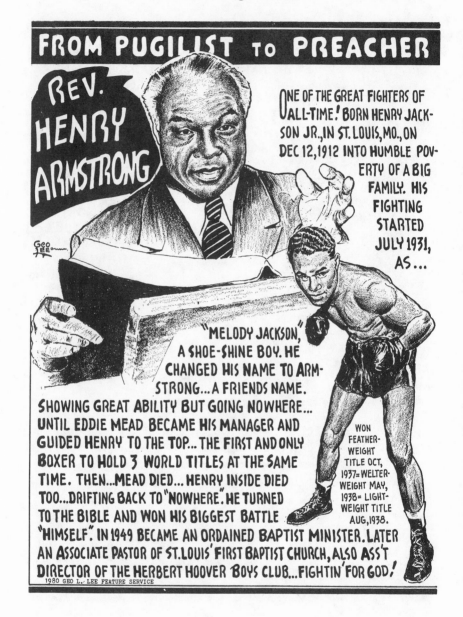

FROM PUGILIST TO PREACHER

REV. HENRY ARMSTRONG

ONE OF THE GREAT FIGHTERS OF ALL-TIME! BORN HENRY JACKSON JR., IN ST. LOUIS, MO., ON DEC 12, 1912 INTO HUMBLE POVERTY OF A BIG FAMILY. HIS FIGHTING STARTED JULY 1931, AS...

GEO LEE

"MELODY JACKSON", A SHOE-SHINE BOY. HE CHANGED HIS NAME TO ARMSTRONG...A FRIENDS NAME. SHOWING GREAT ABILITY BUT GOING NOWHERE... UNTIL EDDIE MEAD BECAME HIS MANAGER AND GUIDED HENRY TO THE TOP... THE FIRST AND ONLY BOXER TO HOLD 3 WORLD TITLES AT THE SAME TIME. THEN...MEAD DIED... HENRY INSIDE DIED TOO...DRIFTING BACK TO "NOWHERE." HE TURNED TO THE BIBLE AND WON HIS BIGGEST BATTLE "HIMSELF." IN 1949 BECAME AN ORDAINED BAPTIST MINISTER. LATER AN ASSOCIATE PASTOR OF ST. LOUIS' FIRST BAPTIST CHURCH, ALSO ASS'T DIRECTOR OF THE HERBERT HOOVER BOYS CLUB...FIGHTIN' FOR GOD!

WON FEATHERWEIGHT TITLE OCT, 1937= WELTERWEIGHT MAY, 1938= LIGHTWEIGHT TITLE AUG, 1938.

1980 GEO L. LEE FEATURE SERVICE

12

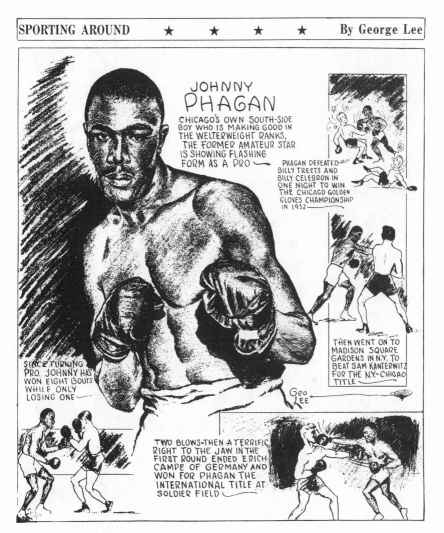

JOHNNY
PHAGAN

CHICAGO'S OWN SOUTH-SIDE
BOY WHO IS MAKING GOOD IN
THE WELTERWEIGHT RANKS,
THE FORMER AMATEUR STAR
IS SHOWING FLASHING
FORM AS A PRO

PHAGAN DEFEATED
BILLY TREETS AND
BILLY CELEBRON IN
ONE NIGHT TO WIN
THE CHICAGO GOLDEN
GLOVES CHAMPIONSHIP
IN 1932

THEN WENT ON TO
MADISON SQUARE
GARDENS IN N.Y. TO
BEAT SAM KANTERWITZ
FOR THE N.Y.-CHIGAO
TITLE

SINCE TURNING
PRO, JOHNNY HAS
WON EIGHT BOUTS
WHILE ONLY
LOSING ONE

Geo
LEE

TWO BLOWS-THEN A TERRIFIC
RIGHT TO THE JAW IN THE
FIRST ROUND ENDED ERICH
CAMPE OF GERMANY AND
WON FOR PHAGAN THE
INTERNATIONAL TITLE AT
SOLDIER FIELD

Chicago Defender   January 27, 1934

13

SPORTING AROUND ★ ★ ★ ★ By George Lee

LEWIS GAVE SLAPSY-MAXIE ROSENBLOOM THE LIGHT HEAVY TITLE HOLDER TWO OF THE WORST DEFEATS OF THE PAST YEAR IN OVER-WEIGHT MATCHES

JOHN HENRY

JOHN HENRY LEWIS FROM PHOENIX ARIZ., WHO FINDS HIMSELF IN THE SPOTLIGHT AS THE LEADING CONTENDER FOR THE LIGHT-HEAVYWEIGHT CROWN

Geo Lee

HELP MA THAT MAN'S HERE AG'IN MAXIE

KAYOED EMMETT ROCCO IN SEVEN ROUNDS

ONE OF THE MOST PROMISING FIGHTER OF THE 1934 SEASON BEAT FRANK ROWSEY-TOM PATRICK AND DREW WITH FRED LENHART

Chicago Defender   February 10, 1934

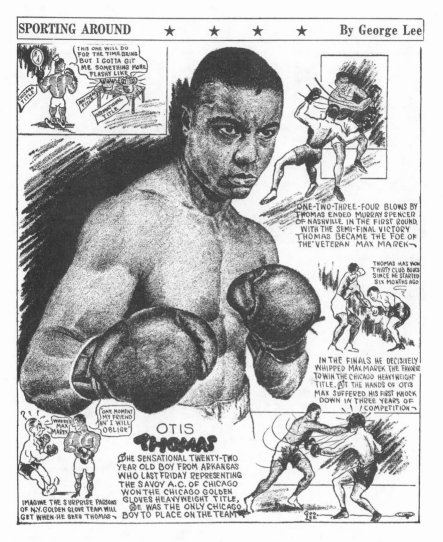

Chicago Defender   March 17, 1934

Chicago Defender   June 2, 1934

Chicago Defender   August 18, 1934

WHEN BOXING wuz BOXING

18 YEARS OF WAITING FOR 36-YEAR OLD ARCHIE AND THEN ON DEC 17, 1952 HE MET JOEY MAXIM LIGHT-HEAVY CHAMP IN ST. LOUIS FOR THE TITLE. A CONTENDER AND 5 YEARS A No. 1

WORLD'S LIGHT HEAVYWEIGHT

Geo LEE

ARCHIE MOORE
WORLD'S LIGHT-HEAVY CHAMP

228 PRO-FIGHTS
140 KNOCKOUTS!

CHALLENGER... FINALLY HIS BIG CHANCE. ARCHIE AN EASY WINNER, GOT THE TITLE AND $800. JOEY RECEIVED $100.000.

BORN IN BENOIT, MISS., DEC 13, 1916 AND RAISED IN ST. LOUIS, MO., HE BEGAN BOXING IN A CCC CAMP IN 1934 AS A MIDDLEWEIGHT. HIS EARLY CAREER WAS FRUSTRATING... HE WAS TOO GOOD! HE VACATED THE TITLE IN 1961 AND FOUGHT HEAVYWEIGHTS. RETIRED 1965.

© 1975 George L. Lee Feature Service

18

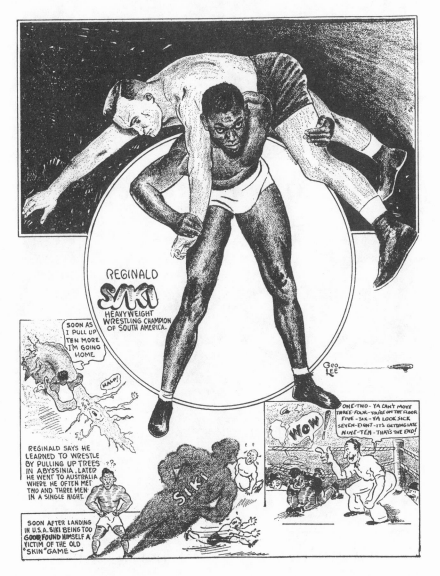

Chicago Defender   December 29, 1934

Chicago Defender   February 16, 1935

Chicago Defender   June 8, 1935

SHOESHINE BOY TO CHAMP AND BACK!

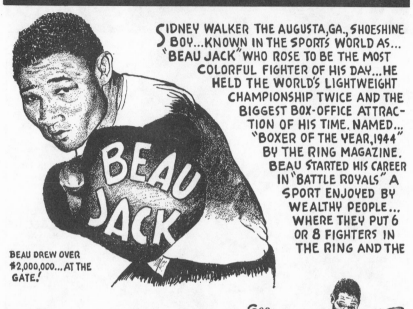

SIDNEY WALKER THE AUGUSTA, GA., SHOESHINE BOY... KNOWN IN THE SPORTS WORLD AS... "BEAU JACK" WHO ROSE TO BE THE MOST COLORFUL FIGHTER OF HIS DAY... HE HELD THE WORLD'S LIGHTWEIGHT CHAMPIONSHIP TWICE AND THE BIGGEST BOX-OFFICE ATTRACTION OF HIS TIME. NAMED... "BOXER OF THE YEAR, 1944" BY THE RING MAGAZINE. BEAU STARTED HIS CAREER IN "BATTLE ROYALS" A SPORT ENJOYED BY WEALTHY PEOPLE... WHERE THEY PUT 6 OR 8 FIGHTERS IN THE RING AND THE

BEAU DREW OVER $2,000,000... AT THE GATE.'

ONE LEFT IS THE WINNER. WHILE WORKING AT THE AUGUSTA NATIONAL GOLF CLUB AS A SHOESHINE BOY HIS ABILITY WAS NOTED AND A FEW MEMBERS BACKED HIM TO TURN PRO IN 1940. ON DEC 18, 1942 HE KO'D TIPPY LARKIN TO WIN THE TITLE. IN 1943 HE LOST IT TO BOB MONTGOMERY AND HE REGAINED IT THE SAME YEAR. FINALLY IN MARCH 1944 HE LOST IT FOR GOOD TO BOB. BEAU FOUGHT ON UNTIL 1951. HE COULD NEITHER READ OR WRITE UNTIL HE WENT INTO THE ARMY IN 1944. HE ENDED BROKE... AND IN 1956 HE WAS SHINING SHOES AGAIN IN MIAMI, FLA.

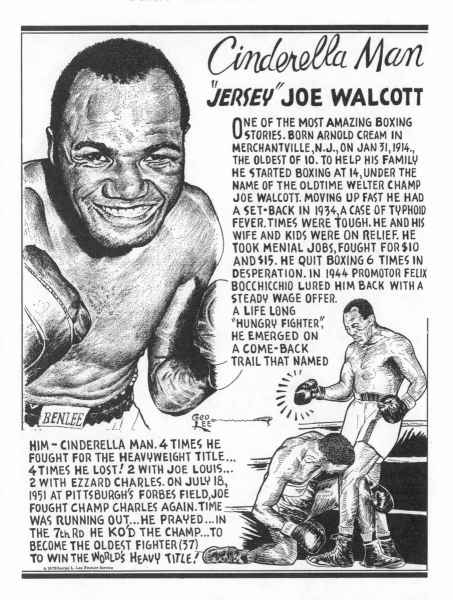

Cinderella Man
"JERSEY" JOE WALCOTT

ONE OF THE MOST AMAZING BOXING STORIES. BORN ARNOLD CREAM IN MERCHANTVILLE, N.J., ON JAN 31, 1914., THE OLDEST OF 10. TO HELP HIS FAMILY HE STARTED BOXING AT 14, UNDER THE NAME OF THE OLDTIME WELTER CHAMP JOE WALCOTT. MOVING UP FAST HE HAD A SET-BACK IN 1934, A CASE OF TYPHOID FEVER. TIMES WERE TOUGH. HE AND HIS WIFE AND KIDS WERE ON RELIEF. HE TOOK MENIAL JOBS, FOUGHT FOR $10 AND $15. HE QUIT BOXING 6 TIMES IN DESPERATION. IN 1944 PROMOTOR FELIX BOCCHICCHIO LURED HIM BACK WITH A STEADY WAGE OFFER. A LIFE LONG "HUNGRY FIGHTER", HE EMERGED ON A COME-BACK TRAIL THAT NAMED

BENLEE

Geo LEE

HIM - CINDERELLA MAN. 4 TIMES HE FOUGHT FOR THE HEAVYWEIGHT TITLE... 4 TIMES HE LOST! 2 WITH JOE LOUIS... 2 WITH EZZARD CHARLES. ON JULY 18, 1951 AT PITTSBURGH'S FORBES FIELD, JOE FOUGHT CHAMP CHARLES AGAIN. TIME WAS RUNNING OUT... HE PRAYED... IN THE 7th RD HE KO'D THE CHAMP...TO BECOME THE OLDEST FIGHTER (37) TO WIN THE WORLD'S HEAVY TITLE!

© 1973 George L. Lee Feature Service

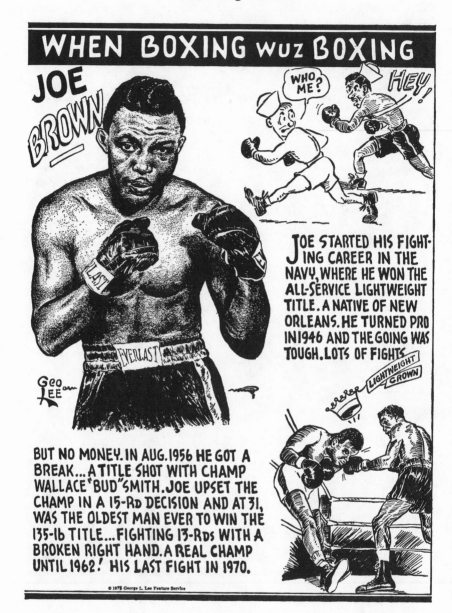

WHEN BOXING wuz BOXING

JOE BROWN

WHO ME?

HEY!

JOE STARTED HIS FIGHTING CAREER IN THE NAVY, WHERE HE WON THE ALL-SERVICE LIGHTWEIGHT TITLE. A NATIVE OF NEW ORLEANS. HE TURNED PRO IN 1946 AND THE GOING WAS TOUGH. LOTS OF FIGHTS

LIGHTWEIGHT CROWN

Geo Lee

BUT NO MONEY. IN AUG. 1956 HE GOT A BREAK... A TITLE SHOT WITH CHAMP WALLACE "BUD" SMITH. JOE UPSET THE CHAMP IN A 15-Rd DECISION AND AT 31, WAS THE OLDEST MAN EVER TO WIN THE 135-lb TITLE... FIGHTING 13-Rds WITH A BROKEN RIGHT HAND. A REAL CHAMP UNTIL 1962! HIS LAST FIGHT IN 1970.

© 1975 George L. Lee Feature Service

WHEN BOXING wuz BOXING

IN 1949 JOE LOUIS RETIRED AS CHAMPION. THE TITLE WAS OPEN...THE NBA RECOGNIZED IN 47 STATES (EXCEPT N.Y.) MATCHED EZZARD CHARLES AND

LOUIS' BEST ROUND WAS THE 10th.

EZZARD CHARLES
OF CINCINNATI
WORLD'S HEAVYWEIGHT CHAMPION

JOE WALCOTT FOR THE TITLE. ON JUNE 22,1949 EZZARD BEAT WALCOTT FOR THE NBA CROWN. LOUIS DECIDES TO COMEBACK FOR HIS TITLE. ON SEPT 27,1950 IN YANKEE STADIUM, CHARLES MET THE ONCE GREAT JOE LOUIS.

..BUT FATHER TIME HAD CAUGHT UP WITH JOE AND A SMASHING RIGHT BY EZ IN THE 14th MADE HIM AN EASY WINNER AND UNDISPUTED HEAVYWEIGHT CHAMPION OF THE WORLD!

Geo Lee

© 1975 George L. Lee Feature Service

25

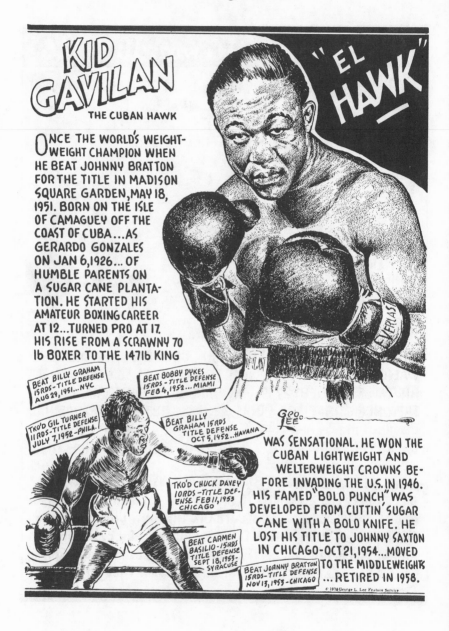

KID GAVILAN
THE CUBAN HAWK

"EL HAWK"

ONCE THE WORLD'S WEIGHT-WEIGHT CHAMPION WHEN HE BEAT JOHNNY BRATTON FOR THE TITLE IN MADISON SQUARE GARDEN, MAY 18, 1951. BORN ON THE ISLE OF CAMAGUEY OFF THE COAST OF CUBA...AS GERARDO GONZALES ON JAN 6, 1926... OF HUMBLE PARENTS ON A SUGAR CANE PLANTATION. HE STARTED HIS AMATEUR BOXING CAREER AT 12...TURNED PRO AT 17. HIS RISE FROM A SCRAWNY 70 lb BOXER TO THE 147 lb KING

BEAT BILLY GRAHAM 15 RDS - TITLE DEFENSE AUG 29, 1951...NYC

BEAT BOBBY DYKES 15 RDS - TITLE DEFENSE FEB 4, 1952...MIAMI

TKO'D GIL TURNER 11 RDS - TITLE DEFENSE JULY 7, 1952 - PHILA.

BEAT BILLY GRAHAM 15 RDS TITLE DEFENSE OCT 5, 1952...HAVANA

TKO'D CHUCK DAVEY 10 RDS - TITLE DEFENSE FEB 11, 1953 CHICAGO

BEAT CARMEN BASILIO - 15 RDS TITLE DEFENSE SEPT 18, 1953 - SYRACUSE

BEAT JOHNNY BRATTON 15 RDS - TITLE DEFENSE NOV 13, 1953 - CHICAGO

Geo. Lee

WAS SENSATIONAL. HE WON THE CUBAN LIGHTWEIGHT AND WELTERWEIGHT CROWNS BEFORE INVADING THE U.S. IN 1946. HIS FAMED "BOLO PUNCH" WAS DEVELOPED FROM CUTTIN' SUGAR CANE WITH A BOLO KNIFE. HE LOST HIS TITLE TO JOHNNY SAXTON IN CHICAGO - OCT 21, 1954...MOVED TO THE MIDDLEWEIGHTS ...RETIRED IN 1958.

© 1978 George L. Lee Feature Service

26

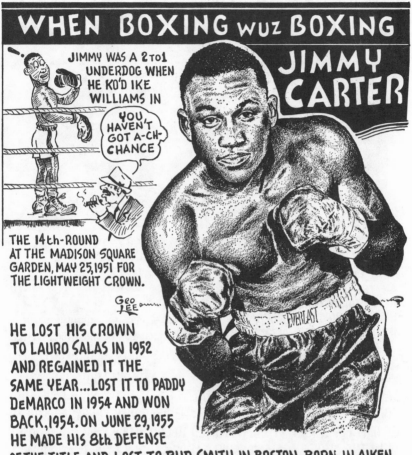

WHEN BOXING wuz BOXING

JIMMY CARTER

JIMMY WAS A 2 to 1 UNDERDOG WHEN HE KO'D IKE WILLIAMS IN

YOU HAVEN'T GOT A-CH-CHANCE

THE 14th-ROUND AT THE MADISON SQUARE GARDEN, MAY 25, 1951 FOR THE LIGHTWEIGHT CROWN.

Geo Lee

HE LOST HIS CROWN TO LAURO SALAS IN 1952 AND REGAINED IT THE SAME YEAR...LOST IT TO PADDY DeMARCO IN 1954 AND WON BACK, 1954. ON JUNE 29, 1955 HE MADE HIS 8th DEFENSE OF THE TITLE AND LOST TO BUD SMITH IN BOSTON. BORN IN AIKEN, S.C., ON DEC 15, 1923...MOVED TO HARLEM AT 9. LEARNED TO BOX AT 14 AT A CATHOLIC BOYS CLUB. LATER IN THE ARMY JIMMY TOOK UP BOXING IN EARNEST. IN 1946 TURNED PRO AND WON 21 STRAIGHT FIGHTS. HIS BIG BREAK...A TITLE MATCH WITH OVERWEIGHT CHAMP WILLIAMS (16 lbs)...IKE MADE 135 lbs...BUT JIMMY WON THE TITLE !

NIGERIA's FIRST WORLD'S CHAMP!

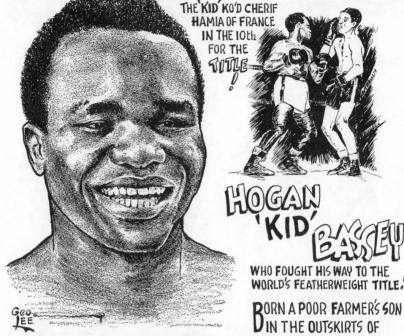

THE 'KID' KO'D CHERIF HAMIA OF FRANCE IN THE 10th FOR THE *TITLE!*

HOGAN 'KID' BASSEY

WHO FOUGHT HIS WAY TO THE WORLD'S FEATHERWEIGHT TITLE!

BORN A POOR FARMER'S SON IN THE OUTSKIRTS OF LAGOS, NIGERIA, ON JUNE 3, 1932. AT 13 HE JOINED A BOYS CLUB AND TOOK UP BOXING. THREE YEARS LATER HE BEAT DICK TURPIN FOR THE NIGERIAN FLYWEIGHT TITLE. HE MOVED TO LIVERPOOL, ENGLAND. IN 1955 HE WON THE EMPIRE CHAMPIONSHIP. SANDY SADDLER THE FEATHERWEIGHT CHAMP VACATED THE TITLE IN 1956...IT WAS OPEN. BASSEY CAME TO THE U.S. AND BEGGED TO ENTER THE FEATHERWEIGHT TOURNAMENT. HE MET AND BEAT MIGUEL BERRIOS IN WASH. D.C... A NEW STAR WAS BORN! IN JUNE 1957 HE MET CHERIF HAMIA...THE PRIDE OF PARIS IN PARIS FOR THE TITLE...HE WON...NIGERIA'S FIRST WORLD CHAMPION!

Geo LEE

FIRST 3-TIME HEAVYWEIGHT CHAMP!

MUHAMMAD ALI

THE FIRST IN BOXING HISTORY TO WIN THE WORLD'S HEAVY-WEIGHT CROWN 3 TIMES. BORN ON JAN 17, 1942 IN LOUISVILLE, KY. CHRISTENED CASSIUS MARCELLUS CLAY II, STARTED CAREER AT 12. WON OLYMPIC LIGHTHEAVY GOLD MEDAL AT ROME IN 1960. TURNED

CASSIUS AT 12

I'M THE GREATEST

PRO OCT 29, 1960. WON TITLE FIRST TIME FEB 25, 1964 FROM SONNY LISTON ON A 7th-RD... TKO, AT MIAMI BEACH. REFUSED ARMY DRAFT (1967) STRIPPED OF TITLE.

REGAINED TITLE, 2nd TIME AT ZAIRE (AFRICA) FROM GEO. FOREMAN... 8-RD KO, OCT 30, 1974... LOST TITLE TO LEON SPINKS-FEB 15, 1978... REGAINED TITLE FOR 3rd-TIME FROM SPINKS AT LAS VEGAS (NEV.) SEPT 15, 1978... WON 15-RDs

Geo LEE

The Story
of
Joe Louis

MAKING OF A CHAMPION

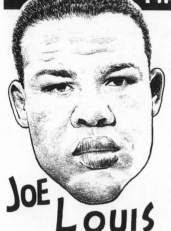

JOE WAS BORN ON MAY 13, 1914 IN LAFAYETTE, ALA. HIS RISE IN THE WORLD OF BOXING, READS LIKE PAGES OF A HORATIO ALGER STORY. FROM A HUMBLE ORIGIN IN ALABAMA AND BOYHOOD DAYS IN DETROIT CAME A YOUTH THAT WAS DESTINED TO BE A SHINING STAR. WHEN JOE WAS 16 A FRIEND AN AMATEUR BOXER TOOK HIM BY THE GYM TO SPAR WITH HIM...JOE LIKED IT

JOE LOUIS

WHO FOUGHT TO THE TOP ...THE WORLD'S HEAVYWEIGHT CHAMPIONSHIP!

Geo Lee

AN' COME OUT FIGHTIN'

DURING HIS AMATEUR CAREER HE FOUGHT 54-TIMES-SCORED 43-KO's-7 DECISIONS-LOST 4!

AND DECIDED HE WOULD BE A BOXER. AT 19 HE ENTERED A TOURNAMENT AS A LIGHT HEAVY. HIS FOE WAS ONE OF THE BEST AMATEURS IN THAT CLASS - JOHNNY MILER, WITH 3-YEARS OF EXPERIENCE AND WINNER OF 7-TOURNAMENTS, JOE WAS FLOORED 7-TIMES BUT EACH TIME GOT UP WITH THE COURAGE THAT CARRIED HIM TO THE TOP...HE LOST HIS FIRST AMATEUR BOUT. MORE DETERMINED THAN EVER HE KO'D HIS NEXT 14 OPPONENTS. HE MET A CLEVER CLINTON BRIDGES AND LOST. IN THE NATIONAL CHAMPIONSHIPS HE LOST-MAX MAREK A NOTRE DAME FOOTBALL PLAYER... BEAT HIM. (1933)

JOE TURNS PRO

JOE WAS RUNNER-UP IN THE NAT'L A.A.U FOR THE LIGHT HEAVY TITLE IN 1933, WHEN MAX MAREK BEAT HIM. IN APRIL OF 1934 HE WON THE A.A.U TITLE AND THE CHICAGO GOLDEN GLOVES CHAMPIONSHIP. HE WAS HAILED AS THE "GREATEST AMATEUR FIGHTER IN THE WORLD"!

ROXBOROUGH

BLACK

JACOBS

BLACKBURN

JOE LOUIS
IN THE BEGINNING~

Geo Lee

FATE SHONE ON LOUIS FROM THE VERY START JOHN ROXBOROUGH OF DETROIT WAS INTERESTED IN HIM AND AGREED TO HANDLE JOE. WITH JULIAN BLACK OF CHICAGO THEY SIGNED TO BE HIS MANAGERS. THEY ACQUIRED JACK BLACKBURN, A SMART FIGHTER WHO HAD FOUGHT THE GREAT JOE GANS, TO BE HIS TRAINER. MIKE JACOBS PROMOTED HIM TO THE TITLE. ON JULY 4, 1934 JOE FOUGHT HIS FIRST PRO FIGHT IN CHICAGO AT BACON'S CASINO... AGAINST JACK KRACKEN. IT LASTED LESS THAN A ROUND... JOE BY A KO! HE EARNED $50. THE LOUIS LEGEND HAD STARTED!

© 1978 George L. Lee Feature Service

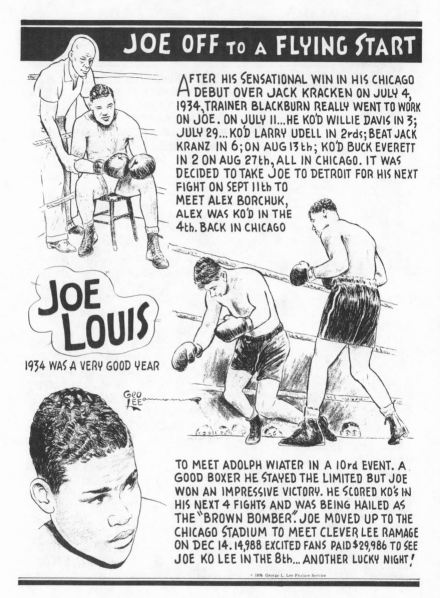

JOE OFF TO A FLYING START

AFTER HIS SENSATIONAL WIN IN HIS CHICAGO DEBUT OVER JACK KRACKEN ON JULY 4, 1934, TRAINER BLACKBURN REALLY WENT TO WORK ON JOE. ON JULY 11...HE KO'D WILLIE DAVIS IN 3; JULY 29...KO'D LARRY UDELL IN 2rds; BEAT JACK KRANZ IN 6; ON AUG 13th; KO'D BUCK EVERETT IN 2 ON AUG 27th, ALL IN CHICAGO. IT WAS DECIDED TO TAKE JOE TO DETROIT FOR HIS NEXT FIGHT ON SEPT 11th TO MEET ALEX BORCHUK, ALEX WAS KO'D IN THE 4th. BACK IN CHICAGO

JOE LOUIS

1934 WAS A VERY GOOD YEAR

TO MEET ADOLPH WIATER IN A 10rd EVENT. A GOOD BOXER HE STAYED THE LIMITED BUT JOE WON AN IMPRESSIVE VICTORY. HE SCORED KO'S IN HIS NEXT 4 FIGHTS AND WAS BEING HAILED AS THE "BROWN BOMBER". JOE MOVED UP TO THE CHICAGO STADIUM TO MEET CLEVER LEE RAMAGE ON DEC 14. 14,988 EXCITED FANS PAID $29,986 TO SEE JOE KO LEE IN THE 8th... ANOTHER LUCKY NIGHT!

34

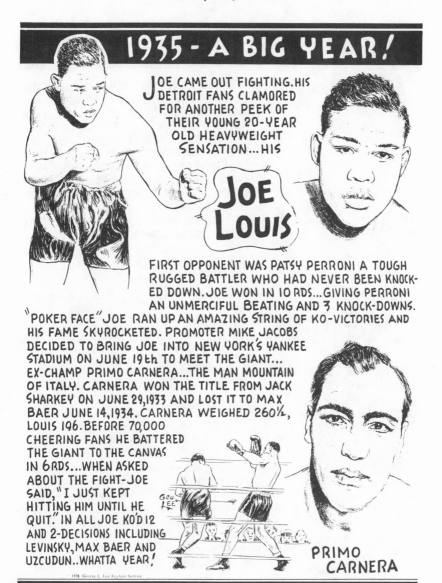

1935 - A BIG YEAR!

JOE CAME OUT FIGHTING. HIS DETROIT FANS CLAMORED FOR ANOTHER PEEK OF THEIR YOUNG 20-YEAR OLD HEAVYWEIGHT SENSATION... HIS

JOE LOUIS

FIRST OPPONENT WAS PATSY PERRONI A TOUGH RUGGED BATTLER WHO HAD NEVER BEEN KNOCKED DOWN. JOE WON IN 10 RDS... GIVING PERRONI AN UNMERCIFUL BEATING AND 3 KNOCK-DOWNS. "POKER FACE" JOE RAN UP AN AMAZING STRING OF KO-VICTORIES AND HIS FAME SKYROCKETED. PROMOTER MIKE JACOBS DECIDED TO BRING JOE INTO NEW YORK'S YANKEE STADIUM ON JUNE 19th TO MEET THE GIANT... EX-CHAMP PRIMO CARNERA...THE MAN MOUNTAIN OF ITALY. CARNERA WON THE TITLE FROM JACK SHARKEY ON JUNE 29,1933 AND LOST IT TO MAX BAER JUNE 14,1934. CARNERA WEIGHED 260½, LOUIS 196. BEFORE 70,000 CHEERING FANS HE BATTERED THE GIANT TO THE CANVAS IN 6 RDS...WHEN ASKED ABOUT THE FIGHT-JOE SAID, "I JUST KEPT HITTING HIM UNTIL HE QUIT." IN ALL JOE KO'D 12 AND 2-DECISIONS INCLUDING LEVINSKY, MAX BAER AND UZCUDUN..WHATTA YEAR!

GEO LEE

PRIMO CARNERA

JOE BEGINS TO SMILE

A S 1936 STARTED, JOE FOUND HIMSELF AT THE TOP OF THE HEAVYWEIGHT DIVISION ANNUAL RATINGS BY THE RING MAGAZINE, EVEN ABOVE CHAMPION JIMMY BRADDOCK FOR HIS OUTSTANDING PEFORMANCES AND WAS GIVEN MOST OF THE CREDIT FOR PUTTING BOXING ON A BIG TIME BASIS. HIS FIGHT WITH MAX BAER BROUGHT BACK THE MILLION DOLLAR GATE. JOE'S FIRST FIGHT OF THE YEAR WAS WITH CHARLEY RETZLAFF ON JAN 17, AT THE CHICAGO STADIUM. RETZLAFF THE 28-YEAR OLD NORTH DAKOTA FARMER HAD A POWERFUL RIGHT BUT WASN'T CONCEDED A CHANCE TO STOP

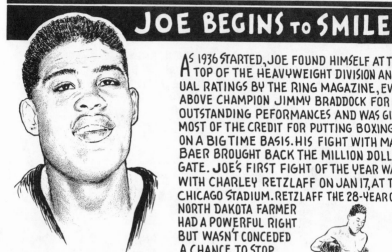

JOE LOUIS

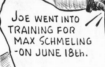

JOE WENT INTO TRAINING FOR MAX SCHMELING -ON JUNE 18th.

THE RISE OF THE BROWN BOMBER. 14,106 FIGHT FANS BRAVED A RAGING BLIZZARD TO SEE JOE LOUIS AND PAID... $67,826.66... JOE'S SHARE $22,566.45. WHEN THE BELL RANG RETZLAFF RUSHED OUT TO MEET JOE AND THREW A HARD RIGHT LANDING ON SHOULDER ANOTHER ON THE HIP OF JOE. LOUIS SHOT A HARD LEFT HOOK...DOWN WENT CHARLEY... HE GOT UP AT 7 ALMOST HELPLESS...JOE SENT A BARRAGE OF BLOWS...THEN A TERRIFIC RIGHT TO THE CHIN! A 1st ROUND KO...1-MIN:25 SECS. HIS 23rd.

JOE TRAINS FOR SCHMELING

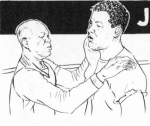

AFTER THE RETZLAFF VICTORY IN JAN., ('36) JOE TOOK A MUCH NEEDED REST. IN MAY, LOUIS WITH TRAINER JACK BLACKBURN AND SPARMATES LEFT FOR LAKEWOOD, N.J., TO TRAIN FOR MAX SCHMELING FROM GERMANY ONCE HEAVYWEIGHT CHAMP (1930-32). IN HIS WORKOUTS JOE APPEARED SLOW BUT IT WAS DIFFICULT FINDING SUITABLE SPARMATES AND HE COULD NOT OPEN UP TOO MUCH. JACK DIDN'T WANT LOUIS TO GET ON EDGE TOO SOON. SCHMELING AND HIS TRAINER MAX MACHON PITCHED THEIR CAMP AT NAPANOCH, N.Y. AND HE WAS WORKING HARD GETTING IN GOOD CONDITION. THE GERMAN WAS CONFIDENT HE COULD BEAT JOE. ON JUNE 8th BLACKBURN STATED THAT HE WASN'T SATISFIED WITH JOE'S FORM. "HE'S STILL SHORT ON BOXING AND IS GETTING HIT TOO OFTEN, BUT HIS TIMING IS IMPROVING." THERE SEEMED TO BE AN AIR OF LEISURE AROUND THE CAMP. JOE WAS PLAYING.....GOLF AND WAS SURE THE GERMAN WOULD BE EASY. HIS POPULARITY FOLLOWED HIM TO LAKEWOOD AND WHENEVER HE APPEARED ON THE STREET THE KIDS FLOCKED AROUND. THE FIGHT WAS SET FOR JUNE 18th AT THE YANKEE STADIUM. BROADWAY HUMMED WITH PRE-FIGHT EXCITEMENT. ODDS...... 4 TO 1 ON JOE. SPORTS WRITERS WERE PICKING HIM TO WIN. WEATHER WAS BAD...NOTHING BUT **RAIN!**

JOE LOUIS

Geo
LEE

© 1976 George L. Lee Feature Service

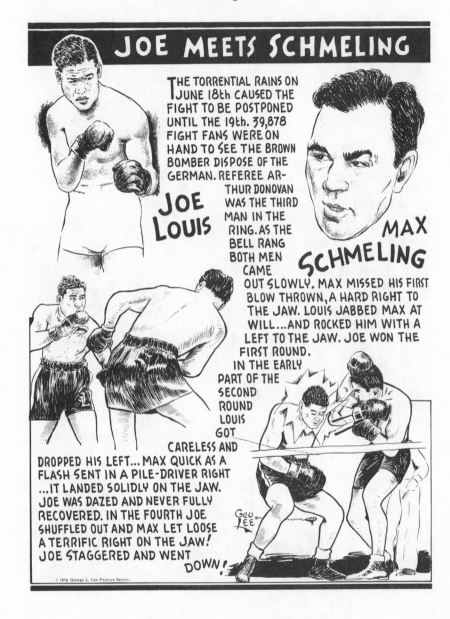

JOE MEETS SCHMELING

JOE LOUIS

MAX SCHMELING

THE TORRENTIAL RAINS ON JUNE 18th CAUSED THE FIGHT TO BE POSTPONED UNTIL THE 19th. 39,878 FIGHT FANS WERE ON HAND TO SEE THE BROWN BOMBER DISPOSE OF THE GERMAN. REFEREE ARTHUR DONOVAN WAS THE THIRD MAN IN THE RING. AS THE BELL RANG BOTH MEN CAME OUT SLOWLY. MAX MISSED HIS FIRST BLOW THROWN, A HARD RIGHT TO THE JAW. LOUIS JABBED MAX AT WILL...AND ROCKED HIM WITH A LEFT TO THE JAW. JOE WON THE FIRST ROUND.

IN THE EARLY PART OF THE SECOND ROUND LOUIS GOT CARELESS AND DROPPED HIS LEFT...MAX QUICK AS A FLASH SENT IN A PILE-DRIVER RIGHT ...IT LANDED SOLIDLY ON THE JAW. JOE WAS DAZED AND NEVER FULLY RECOVERED. IN THE FOURTH JOE SHUFFLED OUT AND MAX LET LOOSE A TERRIFIC RIGHT ON THE JAW! JOE STAGGERED AND WENT DOWN!

Geo Lee

38

JOE'S FIRST DEFEAT

LOUIS WAS DOWN...AT THE COUNT OF TWO HE WAS UP AND BY INSTINCT MANAGED TO GO INTO A CLINCH AS THE BELL ENDED THE ROUND. JOE WEATHERED THE STORM OF BLOWS IN THE 5th AND 6th AND CAME BACK FOR MORE. HE ABSORBED PLENTY

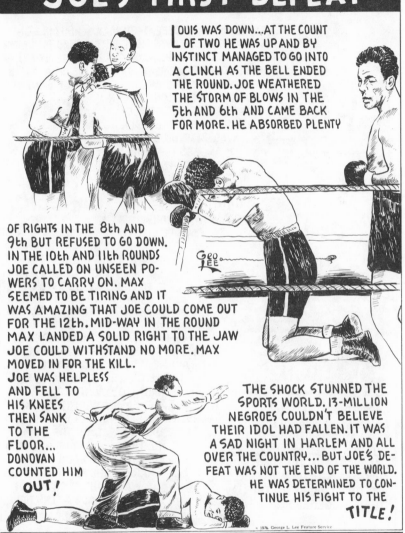

OF RIGHTS IN THE 8th AND 9th BUT REFUSED TO GO DOWN. IN THE 10th AND 11th ROUNDS JOE CALLED ON UNSEEN PO-WERS TO CARRY ON. MAX SEEMED TO BE TIRING AND IT WAS AMAZING THAT JOE COULD COME OUT FOR THE 12th. MID-WAY IN THE ROUND MAX LANDED A SOLID RIGHT TO THE JAW JOE COULD WITHSTAND NO MORE. MAX MOVED IN FOR THE KILL. JOE WAS HELPLESS AND FELL TO HIS KNEES THEN SANK TO THE FLOOR... DONOVAN COUNTED HIM **OUT!**

THE SHOCK STUNNED THE SPORTS WORLD. 13-MILLION NEGROES COULDN'T BELIEVE THEIR IDOL HAD FALLEN. IT WAS A SAD NIGHT IN HARLEM AND ALL OVER THE COUNTRY... BUT JOE'S DE-FEAT WAS NOT THE END OF THE WORLD. HE WAS DETERMINED TO CON-TINUE HIS FIGHT TO THE **TITLE!**

© 1976. George L. Lee Feature Service

39

JOE LOOKS AHEAD in 1936

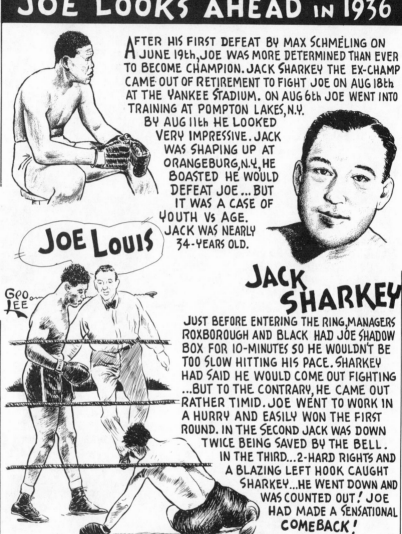

AFTER HIS FIRST DEFEAT BY MAX SCHMELING ON JUNE 19th, JOE WAS MORE DETERMINED THAN EVER TO BECOME CHAMPION. JACK SHARKEY THE EX-CHAMP CAME OUT OF RETIREMENT TO FIGHT JOE ON AUG 18th AT THE YANKEE STADIUM. ON AUG 6th JOE WENT INTO TRAINING AT POMPTON LAKES, N.Y.

BY AUG 11th HE LOOKED VERY IMPRESSIVE. JACK WAS SHAPING UP AT ORANGEBURG, N.Y., HE BOASTED HE WOULD DEFEAT JOE...BUT IT WAS A CASE OF YOUTH Vs AGE. JACK WAS NEARLY 34-YEARS OLD.

JOE LOUIS

GEO LEE

JACK SHARKEY

JUST BEFORE ENTERING THE RING, MANAGERS ROXBOROUGH AND BLACK HAD JOE SHADOW BOX FOR 10-MINUTES SO HE WOULDN'T BE TOO SLOW HITTING HIS PACE. SHARKEY HAD SAID HE WOULD COME OUT FIGHTING ...BUT TO THE CONTRARY, HE CAME OUT RATHER TIMID. JOE WENT TO WORK IN A HURRY AND EASILY WON THE FIRST ROUND. IN THE SECOND JACK WAS DOWN TWICE BEING SAVED BY THE BELL. IN THE THIRD...2-HARD RIGHTS AND A BLAZING LEFT HOOK CAUGHT SHARKEY...HE WENT DOWN AND WAS COUNTED OUT! JOE HAD MADE A SENSATIONAL **COMEBACK!**

© 1976 George L. Lee Feature Service

JOE SMILES AGAIN

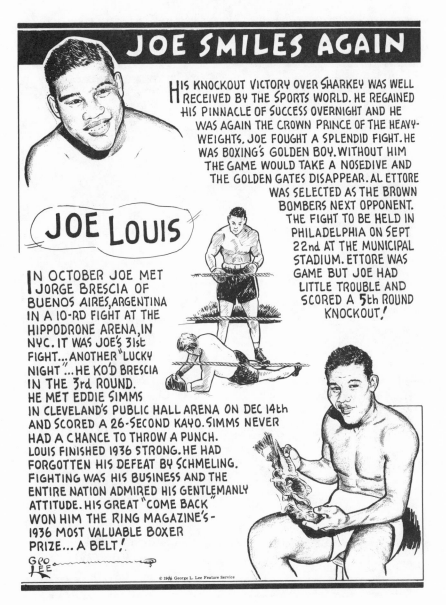

HIS KNOCKOUT VICTORY OVER SHARKEY WAS WELL RECEIVED BY THE SPORTS WORLD. HE REGAINED HIS PINNACLE OF SUCCESS OVERNIGHT AND HE WAS AGAIN THE CROWN PRINCE OF THE HEAVY-WEIGHTS. JOE FOUGHT A SPLENDID FIGHT. HE WAS BOXING'S GOLDEN BOY. WITHOUT HIM THE GAME WOULD TAKE A NOSEDIVE AND THE GOLDEN GATES DISAPPEAR. AL ETTORE WAS SELECTED AS THE BROWN BOMBERS NEXT OPPONENT. THE FIGHT TO BE HELD IN PHILADELPHIA ON SEPT 22nd AT THE MUNICIPAL STADIUM. ETTORE WAS GAME BUT JOE HAD LITTLE TROUBLE AND SCORED A 5th ROUND KNOCKOUT!

JOE LOUIS

IN OCTOBER JOE MET JORGE BRESCIA OF BUENOS AIRES, ARGENTINA IN A 10-RD FIGHT AT THE HIPPODRONE ARENA, IN NYC. IT WAS JOE'S 31st FIGHT... ANOTHER "LUCKY NIGHT"... HE KO'D BRESCIA IN THE 3rd ROUND. HE MET EDDIE SIMMS IN CLEVELAND'S PUBLIC HALL ARENA ON DEC 14th AND SCORED A 26-SECOND KAYO. SIMMS NEVER HAD A CHANCE TO THROW A PUNCH. LOUIS FINISHED 1936 STRONG. HE HAD FORGOTTEN HIS DEFEAT BY SCHMELING. FIGHTING WAS HIS BUSINESS AND THE ENTIRE NATION ADMIRED HIS GENTLEMANLY ATTITUDE. HIS GREAT "COME BACK" WON HIM THE RING MAGAZINE'S - 1936 MOST VALUABLE BOXER PRIZE... A BELT!

GEO LEE

JOE LOUIS - CHAMPION

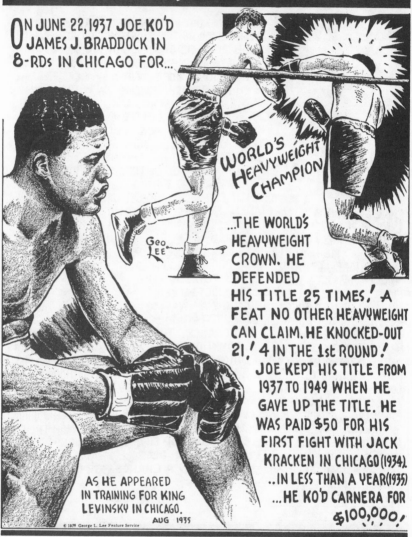

ON JUNE 22, 1937 JOE KO'D JAMES J. BRADDOCK IN 8-RDs IN CHICAGO FOR...

WORLD'S HEAVYWEIGHT CHAMPION

...THE WORLD'S HEAVYWEIGHT CROWN. HE DEFENDED HIS TITLE 25 TIMES! A FEAT NO OTHER HEAVYWEIGHT CAN CLAIM. HE KNOCKED-OUT 21! 4 IN THE 1st ROUND! JOE KEPT HIS TITLE FROM 1937 TO 1949 WHEN HE GAVE UP THE TITLE. HE WAS PAID $50 FOR HIS FIRST FIGHT WITH JACK KRACKEN IN CHICAGO (1934). ..IN LESS THAN A YEAR(1935) ...HE KO'D CARNERA FOR $100,000!

Geo Lee

AS HE APPEARED IN TRAINING FOR KING LEVINSKY IN CHICAGO.
AUG 1935

© 1979 George L. Lee Feature Service

42

1937 - A VERY GOOD YEAR!

AT HIS CAMP IN KENOSHA, WISC., LOUIS WAS VERY IMPRESSIVE...

JOE EARNED $312,250. DURING 1936... A LONG WAY FROM JULY 4, 1934 WHEN HE TURNED PRO FOR $50. AS 1937 OPENED, REPORTS WERE CIRCULATED THAT THE JEWISH PEOPLE WERE GOING TO BOYCOTT THE FIGHT BETWEEN THE CHAMP JAMES J. BRADDOCK AND MAX SCHMELING THE GERMAN. PROMOTERS KNEW THIS WOULD HURT THE GATE AND BEGAN TO THINK ABOUT JOE WITH HIS MILLION DOLLAR GATE APPEAL. IN THE MEANTIME JOE DISPOSED OF STANLEY KETCHELL IN 2-RDS., IN BUFFALO, N.Y. ON JAN 11th. BOB PASTOR OUT-RAN JOE FOR 10-RDS IN THE GARDEN-NYC ON JAN 29th... LOUIS ON A DECISION. KO'D NATIE BROWN IN KANSAS CITY ON FEB 17th. SCHMELING HAD BEEN SIDETRACKED AND THE WAY WAS CLEARED FOR JOE'S

THE CHAMP IN EXCELLENT SHAPE.

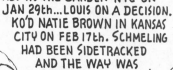

BIG CHANCE... THE WORLD'S HEAVYWEIGHT CROWN ON JUNE 22nd IN COMISKEY PARK, CHICAGO. SIGNING TOOK PLACE ON FEB 19th. BOTH FIGHTERS WENT INTO SERIOUS TRAIN-ING. THE CHAMP AT GRAND BEACH, MICH., AND THE BROWN BOMBER AT KENOSHA, WISC. NOT SINCE 1908 WHEN JACK JOHNSON THE GALVESTON, TEX., WONDER WON THE CHAMPIONSHIP FROM TOMMY BURNS IN SYDNEY, AUSTRALIA ON DEC 26th... HAD A NEGRO BEEN GIVEN A CHANCE FOR THE TITLE!

Geo LEE

JOE LOUIS-WORLD HEAVYWEIGHT CHAMP

CHAMPION JAMES J. BRADDOCK AND CHALLENGER JOE LOUIS WHO WAS THE 2 TO 1 FAVORITE SQUARED OFF IN A 15-ROUND TITLE FIGHT ON JUNE 22, 1937 IN COMISKEY PARK, CHICAGO. JOE WAS 23, BRADDOCK 32. 55,000 FANS PAID OVER A HALF-MILLION TO SEE THE CHAMP THROW A SURPRISE... TERRIFIC RIGHT IN THE FIRST ROUND THAT FLOORED JOE... HE WAS UP WITHOUT A COUNT. FROM THEN ON LOUIS FOUGHT A BRILLIANT FIGHT. BRADDOCK A GAME FIGHTER THREW PUNCHES AS LONG AS HE COULD...BUT JOE'S SMASHING ATTACK WAS TOO MUCH AND IN THE 8th ROUND A LONG RIGHT TO THE CHAMP'S JAW... HE CRASHED TO THE CANVAS, HE NEVER HEARD THE COUNT - "THE WINNAH AN' NEW HEAVYWEIGHT CHAMPEEN OF THE WORLD."

JOE LOUIS

CHAMP

Geo LEE

© 1976 George L. Lee Feature Service

Boxing
Events
of the '50s

Chicago Tribune   February 11, 1951

Jake LaMotta, the 160 pound titleholder for 20 months, was defeated in the 13th round.

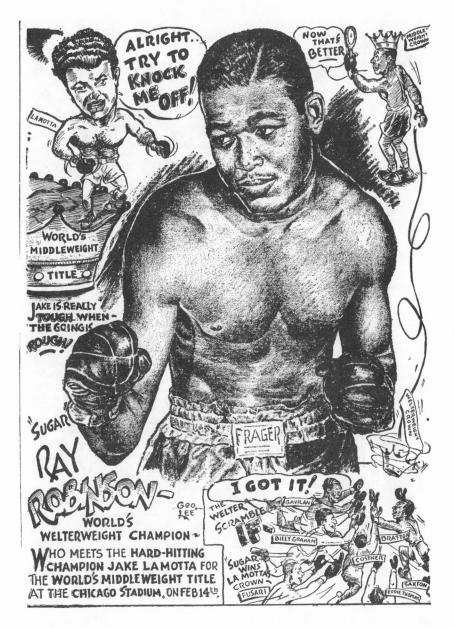

Chicago Defender   November 25, 1950

Louis scored a decisive victory over Cesar Brion in a 10-round fight.

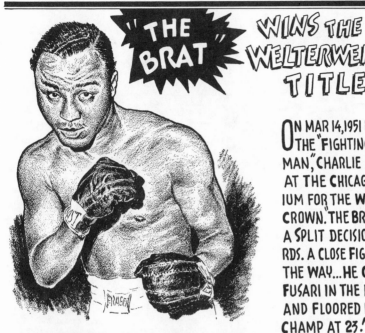

"THE BRAT"

WINS THE WELTERWEIGHT TITLE!

ON MAR 14,1951 HE MET THE "FIGHTING MILKMAN," CHARLIE FUSARI AT THE CHICAGO STADIUM FOR THE WELTER CROWN. THE BRAT "WON A SPLIT DECISION IN 15-RDS. A CLOSE FIGHT ALL THE WAY... HE CAUGHT FUSARI IN THE 10th RD AND FLOORED HIM. A CHAMP AT 23! HIS

JOHNNY BRATTON

Geo LEE

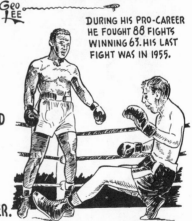

DURING HIS PRO-CAREER HE FOUGHT 88 FIGHTS WINNING 63. HIS LAST FIGHT WAS IN 1955.

GLORY WAS SHORT... HE LOST HIS CROWN TO KID GAVILAN ON MAY 15, 1951 AND NEVER REGAINED IT. BORN IN LITTLE ROCK, ARK., (1927) AND RAISED IN CHICAGO. STARTED BOXING AT 15... WON 120 OF 130 AMATEUR. BOUTS. WON THE 1944 GOLDEN GLOVES LIGHTWEIGHT TITLE. A CLEVER BOXER AND TERRIFIC PUNCHER... BUT AN ERRATIC PERFORMER.

Chicago Defender   May 26, 1951

Ezzard Charles retained his title in a 15-round fight by unanimous vote of the officials.

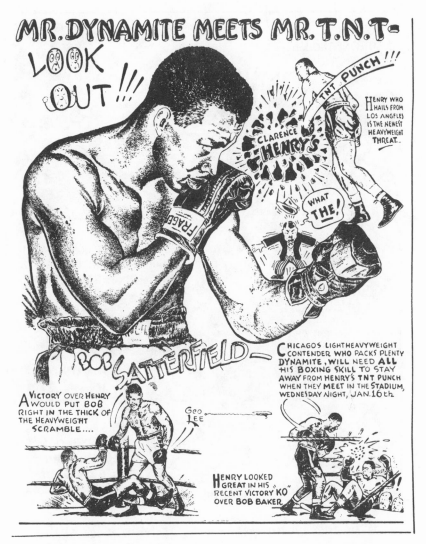

Chicago Defender   January 12, 1952

Satterfield was knocked out by Clarence Henry in the first round.

Chicago Defender   March 22, 1952

Williams was defeated in the fifth round.

Chicago Tribune   April 14, 1952

Sugar Ray Robinson defeated Rocky Graziano.

Chicago Tribune   October 11, 1952

Jimmy Carter received a well-earned 15-round decision over Lauro Salas.

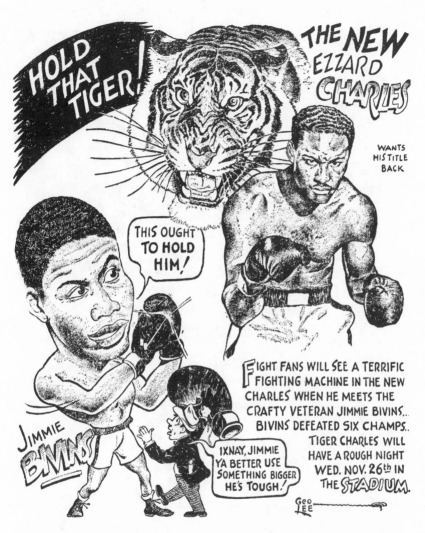

Chicago Defender   November 22, 1952

Chicago Defender March 21, 1953

Marciano knocked out Walcott in a 15-round bout.

WALCOTT GUNS FOR ROCKY'S TITLE

Chicago Defender   May 9, 1953

Rocky Marciano scored a knockout in 2:25 of the first round.

Chicago Defender   November 5, 1953

Kid Gavilan, welterweight champion, retained his title in a 15-round victory over Johnny Bratton.

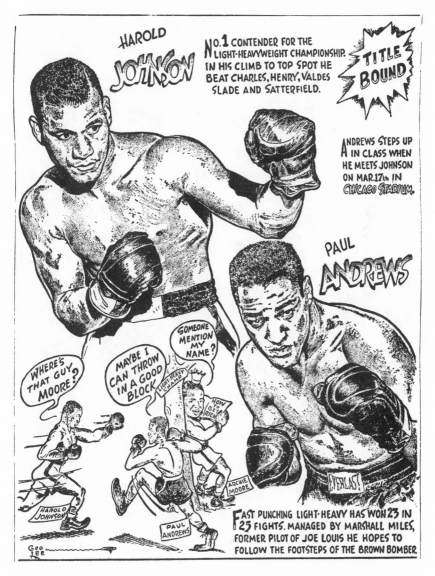

Chicago Defender   March 13, 1954

Harold Johnson knocked out Andrews in the sixth round.

Chicago Defender   March 20, 1954

In a close match, Bobo Olson saved his middle weight championship from Kid Gavilan.

Chicago Defender   September 25, 1954

Andrews lost to Johnson in the sixth round.

Chicago Defender   October 15, 1955

Robinson came back to win the championship in a two-round knockout.

WELTERWEIGHT CHAMP OF THE WORLD RETAINED HIS CROWN AGAINST ROUGH, TOUGH TONY DEMARCO IN 1955, THE FIGHT OF THE YEAR!

CARMEN BASILIO

CHICAGO STADIUM BOUT MARCH 14th LOOMS AS ANOTHER FIGHT OF THE YEAR. WITH BASILIO GOING ALL OUT TO KEEP HIS CROWN!

WHERE'S MY CROWN? JOHNNY SAXTON

SAXTON WON THE TITLE FROM KID GAVILAN IN 1954. HE IS DETERMINED TO WIN IT BACK.

Geo LEE

Chicago Defender   March 10, 1956

Saxton won over Basilio by unanimous decision.

Chicago Defender   November 30, 1956

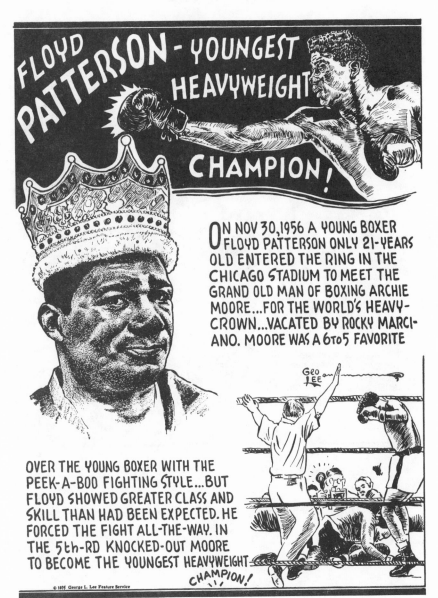

FLOYD PATTERSON - YOUNGEST HEAVYWEIGHT CHAMPION!

ON NOV 30,1956 A YOUNG BOXER FLOYD PATTERSON ONLY 21-YEARS OLD ENTERED THE RING IN THE CHICAGO STADIUM TO MEET THE GRAND OLD MAN OF BOXING ARCHIE MOORE...FOR THE WORLD'S HEAVY-CROWN...VACATED BY ROCKY MARCIANO. MOORE WAS A 6ᴛᴏ5 FAVORITE

OVER THE YOUNG BOXER WITH THE PEEK-A-BOO FIGHTING STYLE...BUT FLOYD SHOWED GREATER CLASS AND SKILL THAN HAD BEEN EXPECTED. HE FORCED THE FIGHT ALL-THE-WAY. IN THE 5th-RD KNOCKED-OUT MOORE TO BECOME THE YOUNGEST HEAVYWEIGHT CHAMPION!

© 1975 George L. Lee Feature Service

65

Chicago Defender   May 12, 1956

Saxton scored a technical knockout over Turner in the tenth round.

Chicago Defender   November 30, 1957

Brown knocked out Lopes in the 11th round.

International Boxing Club   March 1958

MAR 25, 1958 SUGAR RAY WINS MIDDLEWEIGHT TITLE FOR 5th TIME!

RAY ROBINSON REGAINED HIS TITLE WHEN HE WON A SPLIT-DECISION OVER CHAMP CARMEN BASILIO IN 15-RDS AT CHICAGO STADIUM. "SUGAR RAY" THE DANCING MASTER WHO BATTLED HIS WAY TO THE WELTERWEIGHT CROWN AND MIDDLEWEIGHT CROWN 4-TIMES AND LOST ONLY 6 OF 149 BOUTS IN 17-YEARS OF BOXING WAS THE FIRST TO WIN THE MIDDLEWEIGHT TITLE 5-TIMES...BEFORE THE LARGEST PAID AUDIENCE IN BOXING HISTORY-375,000 TV-FANS...17,976 AT THE STADIUM!

BUT I COULDN'T SEE AFTER THE 4TH ROUND!

SORRY ABOUT THAT CARMEN.

A SMASHING RIGHT IN THE 5th CLOSED BASILIO'S LEFT EYE.

© 1976 George L. Lee Feature Service

69

Baseball
Players

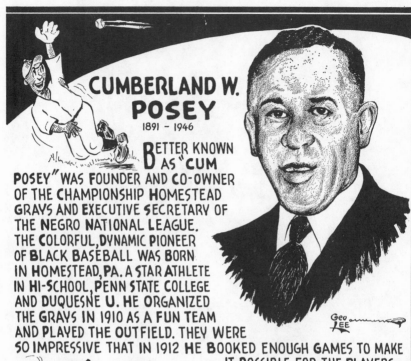

CUMBERLAND W. POSEY
1891 – 1946

BETTER KNOWN AS "CUM POSEY" WAS FOUNDER AND CO-OWNER OF THE CHAMPIONSHIP HOMESTEAD GRAYS AND EXECUTIVE SECRETARY OF THE NEGRO NATIONAL LEAGUE. THE COLORFUL, DYNAMIC PIONEER OF BLACK BASEBALL WAS BORN IN HOMESTEAD, PA. A STAR ATHLETE IN HI-SCHOOL, PENN STATE COLLEGE AND DUQUESNE U. HE ORGANIZED THE GRAYS IN 1910 AS A FUN TEAM AND PLAYED THE OUTFIELD. THEY WERE SO IMPRESSIVE THAT IN 1912 HE BOOKED ENOUGH GAMES TO MAKE IT POSSIBLE FOR THE PLAYERS TO DEVOTE FULL-TIME, PLAYING BASEBALL. IN THE EARLY 20'S THE GRAYS JOINED THE NEGRO NATIONAL LEAGUE AND BECAME A TOP TEAM. IN 1929 CUM GAVE UP PLAYING AND MANAGED THE TEAM. AFTER A FEW YEARS HE TOOK OVER THE BUSINESS END. FROM 1937–1946 THEY WON 8 OF 9 CHAMPIONSHIPS. UNDER HIS LEADERSHIP BLACK BASE-BALL PROSPERED. HE ESTABLISHED THE ALL-STARS vs MAJOR LEAGUERS.

CUM DEVELOPED MANY GREAT PLAYERS.

© 1972 George L. Lee Feature Service

72

Chicago Defender   May 12, 1934

Chicago Defender   May 26, 1934

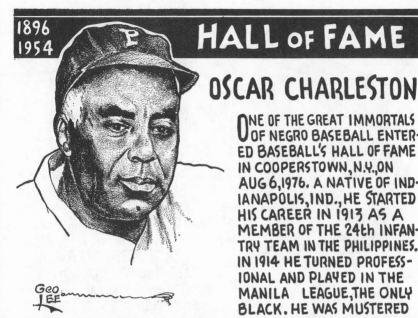

HALL of FAME

1896
1954

OSCAR CHARLESTON

ONE OF THE GREAT IMMORTALS OF NEGRO BASEBALL ENTERED BASEBALL'S HALL OF FAME IN COOPERSTOWN, N.Y., ON AUG 6, 1976. A NATIVE OF INDIANAPOLIS, IND., HE STARTED HIS CAREER IN 1913 AS A MEMBER OF THE 24th INFANTRY TEAM IN THE PHILIPPINES. IN 1914 HE TURNED PROFESSIONAL AND PLAYED IN THE MANILA LEAGUE, THE ONLY BLACK. HE WAS MUSTERED

Geo. LEE

OUT OF THE ARMY IN 1915 AND SIGNED WITH THE INDIANAPOLIS A.B.C's UNTIL 1918, THEN TO THE CHICAGO AMERICAN GIANTS UNDER THE GUIDING GENIUS OF RUBE FOSTER. A GREAT CENTERFIELDER AND FIRST BASEMAN. FROM 1920 TO 1940 HE PLAYED WITH SUCH TEAMS AS THE ST. LOUIS GIANTS, INPLS A.B.C, HARRISBURG, HILLDALE, HOMESTEAD GRAYS, PITTSBURGH AND TOLEDO CRAWFORDS. IN 1941 SIGNED AS PLAYER-MANAGER OF PHILA., STARS UNTIL HE RETIRED IN 1950.

PLAYING WITH HARRISBURG IN 1925 HE LED THE EASTERN NEGRO LEAGUE WITH A 430 AVG.!

IN 1929 HIT .396 TO LEAD THE AMERICAN NEGRO LEAGUE!

357

A TERRIFIC HITTER WITH A LIFETIME .357 AVG!

"GENTLEMAN DAVE"

MALARCHER

TRULY ONE OF BLACK BASEBALLS ALL-TIME GREATS. HE EXCELLED AT 3rd BASE...A BRILLIANT INFIELDER, A GOOD HITTER (LIFE-TIME AV. 347), A DARING BASE RUNNER. AS MANAGER OF CHICAGO AMERICAN GIANTS HE WAS GREAT. HIGHLY RESPECTED BY ALL IN BASEBALL, SPORTSWRITERS CALLED HIM "GENTLEMAN DAVE." A PROLIFIC WRITER OF POEMS AND A REAL ESTATE BROKER. BORN ON OCT 18, 1894 IN WHITEHALL, LA., THE YOUNGEST OF 11. ENTERED ELEMENTARY SCHOOL OF NEW ORLEANS UNIV. (LATER DILLARD U.). STARTED HIS BASEBALL CAREER WHILE IN COLLEGE, PLAYING WITH THE NEW

Geo LEE

ORLEANS EAGLES A SEMI-PRO TEAM (1914-15). IN 1916 PLAYED 3rd BASE FOR THE INDIANAPOLIS ABC's. IN 1918 SERVED IN ARMY IN W.W. I. IN 1919 PLAYED WITH THE DETROIT STARS. JOINED THE CHGO. AMERICAN GIANTS, 1920-35. RETIRED TO DEVOTE FULL-TIME TO HIS REAL ESTATE BUSINESS, CIVIC AND RELIGIOUS WORK. DIED AT 87 (MAY 11, '82)

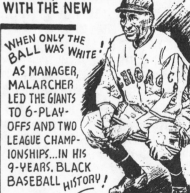

WHEN ONLY THE BALL WAS WHITE!
AS MANAGER, MALARCHER LED THE GIANTS TO 6-PLAY-OFFS AND TWO LEAGUE CHAMPIONSHIPS...IN HIS 9-YEARS. BLACK BASEBALL HISTORY!

1985 GEO L. LEE FEATURE SERVICE

Chicago Defender   April 7, 1934

JOSH GIBSON

1911 – 1947

FAMOUS HOMESTEAD GRAYS' (PA) SLUGGING CATCHER WAS BORN IN BUENA VISTA, GA. HIS FAMILY MOVED TO PITTSBURGH PA., HE STARTED HIS BASEBALL CAREER WITH THE PITTSBURGH CRAWFORDS AT 16 (1927). IN 1930 -31 SEASON HE PLAYED WITH THE HOMESTEAD GRAYS. JOSH RETURNED TO THE CRAWFORDS TO TEAM UP WITH SATCHEL PAIGE IN 1932 AND STAYED UNTIL 1936. BACK TO THE GRAYS IN 1937 WHERE HE WAS OUTSTANDING UNTIL HIS DEATH IN 1947. HE LED THE NEGRO NAT'L

Geo LEE

LEAGUE WITH AN AV. OF .393 IN 1945. JOSH WAS THE HOME-RUN KING OF NEGRO BASEBALL...HE ONCE HIT A HOMER 513-FT IN 1930 AT MONESSEN, PA. HIS NAME IS ENSHRINED IN BASEBALL'S HALL OF FAME. HIT FIRST HOMER IN LEFT-FIELD BLEACHERS IN THE YANKEE STADIUM. (1930)

84 HOME-RUNS IN ONE SEASON!

Chicago Defender   April 21, 1934

SPORTING AROUND ★ ★ ★ ★ **By George Lee**

WHEN LARRY MISSES TAGGIN' 'EM OUT AT THE PLATE IT WILL BE TIME TO FIGURE HE'S THRU. ONLY THREE RUNNERS HAVE ESCAPED HIM IN FIFTEEN YEARS OF PLAYING

A TRIFLE DELAYED BUT HERE I AM,

LIKE MOST CATCHERS IS SLOW ON THE BASES. HE HIT A BALL AGAINST THE CENTER FIELD FENCE IN THE EAST-WEST ALL-STAR GAME BUT WAS THROWN OUT ATTEMPTING TO STRETCH IT INTO A HOMER. A PLAY ANY OTHER PLAYER COULD HAVE EASILY COMPLETED

SOCK IT IN!

SURE BALL SNATCHER LARRY HASN'T HAD A PASSED BALL IN FIVE YEARS

"MEMPHIS LARRY BROWN"

BRILLIANT CATCHER FOR THE CHICAGO AMERICAN GIANTS WHO FOR THE LAST EIGHT YEARS HAS SENSATIONALLY HELD THE TITLE OF THE WORLD'S GREATEST CATCHER

IF HE WAS ONLY WHITE JOHN J. McGRAW

THE LATE JOHN McGRAW MANAGER OF THE N.Y. GIANTS ONCE MADE THE COMMENT OF LARRY SAYING "IF HE WAS ONLY WHITE, HE'D BE WORTH A MILLION BUCKS"

Geo Lee

Chicago Defender   June 16, 1934

Chicago Defender   June 16, 1934

Chicago Defender   July 21, 1934

Chicago Defender   April 21, 1934

CAMPY

ROY CAMPANELLA

THE FIRST CATCHER EVER TO HIT 20 OR MORE HOMERS IN 3-SUCCESSIVE YEARS (1949-50-51). WAS BORN ON NOV. 19, 1921 IN HOMESTEAD, PA. HE STARTED HIS BASEBALL CAREER AT 15. BIG FOR HIS AGE, THE MANAGER OF THE BACHARACH GIANTS OF PHILA., IN THE NEGRO LEAGUES ASKED HIM TO PLAY ON A WEEKEND TRIP. WHILE IN NEW YORK CITY, THE BALTI-MORE ELITES OFFERED HIM $60-A-MONTH, HE ACCEPTED (1937). DURING HIS EARLY YEARS HE WOULD PLAY ALL YEAR. IN THE WINTER IN CUBA AND PUERTO RICO. DURABLE, HE CAUGHT A DOUBLE HEADER FOR THE ELITES MORE THAN ONCE. THE MAJOR LEAGUE COLOR-LINE WAS ABOUT TO BE BROKEN BY BRANCH RICKEY OF THE BROOKLYN DODGERS WHEN HE SENT JACKIE ROBINSON TO MONTREAL IN 1946. RICKEY SIGNED CAMPY TO THEIR CLASS-B TEAM IN NASHUA, NEW HAMP. THE SAME YEAR. IN 1947 CAMPY WENT TO MONTREAL, THEN TO ST. PAUL (1948) IN THE AMERICAN ASSOC., THE FIRST BLACK. HE WAS GREAT AND THE DODGERS IN A SLUMP CALLED HIM UP... JULY 2, 1948. THE SECOND BLACK IN THE MAJOR LEAGUES. THE MOST VALUABLE PLAYER IN THE NATIONAL LEAGUE, 3-TIMES (1951-53-55). IN JAN 1958 TRAGEDY STRUCK... A CAR ACCIDENT LEFT HIM PARALYZED FROM THE NECK DOWN. A GREAT CAREER ENDED... BUT NOT FORGOTTEN. IN 1969 HE WAS VOTED INTO BASEBALL'S **HALL OF FAME!**

Geo. Lee

© 1974 George L. Lee Feature Service

I FEEL GREAT...IF IT WASN'T FOR THIS SPRAINED WRIST AND PULLED LEG MUSCLES AND BACK MISERY ...BETCHA I COULD HIT 50 HOMERS

BIG LUKE, HOW DO YOU FEEL?

WHEN BIG LUKE WAS HEALTHY HE WAS 235 lbs OF REAL POWER....

LUKE EASTER

A BIG BAT...BUT PLAGUED WITH INJURIES.

Geo LEE

CLEVELAND INDIANS' BIG FIRST BASEMAN WASN'T TOO FAST A-FIELD ...BUT COULD HIT. BORN IN ST. LOUIS ON AUG 4, 1921. AS A BOY HE ONLY PLAYED SOFTBALL. IN 1941 HE WAS IN A CAR ACCIDENT WHICH LEFT HIM WITH TWO BROKEN LEGS. HE SPENT 13-MONTHS IN THE ARMY. BY 1945 HE HAD DECIDED TO BE A BALLPLAYER. STARTED AT $18-A-WEEK. ABE SAPERSTEIN SAW HIM AND SIGNED LUKE TO THE CINCINNATI CRESCENTS. IN 1947 HE WENT TO THE HOME-STEAD GRAYS...THE INDIANS SIGNED HIM FOR THEIR SAN DIEGO TEAM IN 1949 WHERE HE HIT .363...92-RBI's...25 HR's..ON TO THE MAJORS AND CLEVELAND. HE NEVER REACHED HIS POTENTIAL DUE TO INJURIES. BACK TO SAN DIEGO IN 1954. A HEALTHY LUKE WOULD HAVE BEEN GREAT!

IN 1950 HE PLAYED IN 141-GAMES- 28 HRs .280 AV -107 RBI's

I HOPE HE STAYS HEALTHY

YEA

....WALLS CAME TUMBLING DOWN

JACKIE ROBINSON

ON THE NIGHT OF OCT 23,1945 THE EX-**UCLA** FOOTBALL ACE AND **U.S.** ARMY LIEUTENANT SIGNED A BASE- BALL CONTRACT WITH THE MONTREAL ROYALS OF THE INTERNATIONAL LEAGUE AND THE FARM TEAM OF THE BROOKLYN DODGERS (NL).THE SIGNING TOOK PLACE IN MONTREAL (CANADA) AND JACKIE BECAME THE FIRST NEGRO ADMITTED TO MODERN ORGANIZED BASEBALL.

Geo LEE

THE HISTORIC EVENT OPENED THE DOOR TO BLACK PLAYERS.

1919 1972

ON APRIL 18,1946 JACKIE MADE HIS DEBUT AGAINST THE JERSEY CITY GIANTS (NJ). BEFORE 50,000 HE MADE BASE- BALL HISTORY IN A GREAT BIG WAY... 4-HITS INCLUDING A 2- ON HOMER... 4-RUNS SCORED... STOLE 2-BASES AND 4-RBI's. THE ROYALS WON 14-1. HIS FIRST SEASON OVER... HE HAD WON THE. INT'L LEAGUE BATTING CROWN!

G	AB	R	H	2B	3B	HR	RBI	SB
124	144	113	155	25	8	3	65	40

PCT-.349!

© 1976, George L. Lee Feature Service

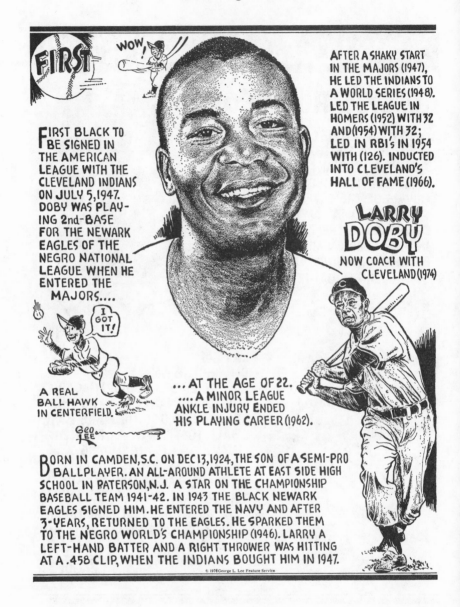

FIRST

WOW!

FIRST BLACK TO BE SIGNED IN THE AMERICAN LEAGUE WITH THE CLEVELAND INDIANS ON JULY 5, 1947. DOBY WAS PLAYING 2nd-BASE FOR THE NEWARK EAGLES OF THE NEGRO NATIONAL LEAGUE WHEN HE ENTERED THE MAJORS....

AFTER A SHAKY START IN THE MAJORS (1947), HE LED THE INDIANS TO A WORLD SERIES (1948). LED THE LEAGUE IN HOMERS (1952) WITH 32 AND (1954) WITH 32; LED IN RBI's IN 1954 WITH (126). INDUCTED INTO CLEVELAND'S HALL OF FAME (1966).

LARRY DOBY

NOW COACH WITH CLEVELAND (1974)

I GOT IT!

A REAL BALL HAWK IN CENTERFIELD.

GEO LEE

... AT THE AGE OF 22. .... A MINOR LEAGUE ANKLE INJURY ENDED HIS PLAYING CAREER (1962).

BORN IN CAMDEN, S.C. ON DEC 13, 1924, THE SON OF A SEMI-PRO BALLPLAYER. AN ALL-AROUND ATHLETE AT EAST SIDE HIGH SCHOOL IN PATERSON, N.J. A STAR ON THE CHAMPIONSHIP BASEBALL TEAM 1941-42. IN 1943 THE BLACK NEWARK EAGLES SIGNED HIM. HE ENTERED THE NAVY AND AFTER 3-YEARS, RETURNED TO THE EAGLES. HE SPARKED THEM TO THE NEGRO WORLD'S CHAMPIONSHIP (1946). LARRY A LEFT-HAND BATTER AND A RIGHT THROWER WAS HITTING AT A .458 CLIP, WHEN THE INDIANS BOUGHT HIM IN 1947.

MAJOR LEAGUE MANAGER

LARRY DOBY

ON JUNE 30,1978 HE BECAME THE MANAGER OF THE CHICAGO WHITE SOX THE SECOND BLACK IN THE MAJORS. A NATIVE OF CAMDEN, S.C., HE PLAYED WITH CLEVELAND AND THE WHITE SOX, RETIRING AT THE END OF 1959. A FINE OUTFIELDER, HE HIT 253-HOMERS AND HAD A CAREER .283 BATTING AV. A BATTING COACH FOR THE EXPO'S OF MONTREAL WHEN VEECK SIGNED HIM IN 1976 AS BATTING COACH FOR THE SOX. NOW 53, DOBY HAS BEEN IN BASEBALL FOR 31-YEARS!

LARRY WAS PLAYING WITH THE NEWARK EAGLES OF THE NEGRO LEAGUE AND HITTING .458 WHEN BILL VEECK BOUGHT HIM FOR $15,000 FOR THE CLEVELAND INDIANS. ON JULY 5,1947 HE BECAME THE FIRST BLACK IN THE MAJOR'S AMERICAN LEAGUE!

1978 GEO L. LEE FEATURE SERVICE

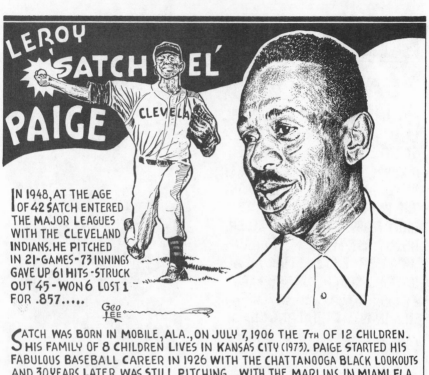

IN 1948, AT THE AGE OF 42 SATCH ENTERED THE MAJOR LEAGUES WITH THE CLEVELAND INDIANS. HE PITCHED IN 21-GAMES-73 INNINGS GAVE UP 61 HITS -STRUCK OUT 45 - WON 6 LOST 1 FOR .857.....

Geo LEE

SATCH WAS BORN IN MOBILE, ALA., ON JULY 7, 1906 THE 7TH OF 12 CHILDREN. HIS FAMILY OF 8 CHILDREN LIVES IN KANSAS CITY (1973). PAIGE STARTED HIS FABULOUS BASEBALL CAREER IN 1926 WITH THE CHATTANOOGA BLACK LOOKOUTS AND 30 YEARS LATER WAS STILL PITCHING...WITH THE MARLINS IN MIAMI, FLA. DURING THAT PERIOD HE WAS IN THE NEGRO LEAGUES, MEXICO, SO. AMERICA AND BECAME AN OUTSTANDING BOX OFFICE ATTRACTION. HOWEVER THE COLOR-LINE KEPT HIM OUT OF THE MAJORS UNTIL HE HAD PAST HIS REAL GREATNESS...

I'LL USE MY HESITATION BALL!

PITCHING FOR THE PITTSBURG CRAWFORDS IN 1936 HE PITCHED 5 - 9 INNING GAMES IN 1 WEEK-WON ALL 5...GAVE UP ONLY 3-RUNS.

SATCH STRUCK OUT THE GREAT HORNSBY 5-TIMES IN 1-GAME.

PAIGE ENTERED BASEBALL'S HALL OF FAME-AUG, 1971. A GREAT TRIBUTE TO A GREAT PITCHER.

HALL OF FAME COOPERSTOWN N.Y.

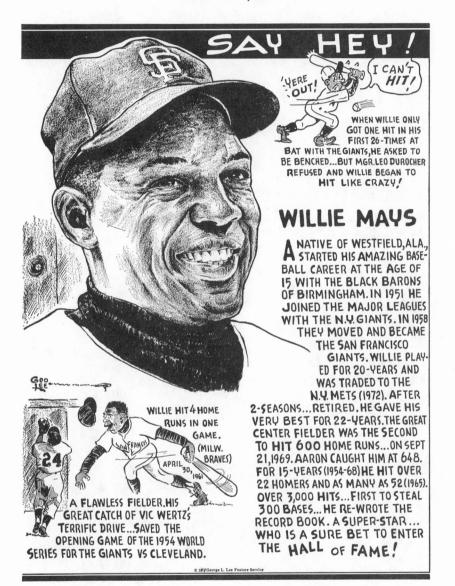

SAY HEY!

'YERE OUT! I CAN'T HIT!

WHEN WILLIE ONLY GOT ONE HIT IN HIS FIRST 26-TIMES AT BAT WITH THE GIANTS, HE ASKED TO BE BENCHED...BUT MGR. LEO DUROCHER REFUSED AND WILLIE BEGAN TO HIT LIKE CRAZY!

WILLIE MAYS

A NATIVE OF WESTFIELD, ALA., STARTED HIS AMAZING BASE-BALL CAREER AT THE AGE OF 15 WITH THE BLACK BARONS OF BIRMINGHAM. IN 1951 HE JOINED THE MAJOR LEAGUES WITH THE N.Y. GIANTS. IN 1958 THEY MOVED AND BECAME THE SAN FRANCISCO GIANTS. WILLIE PLAY-ED FOR 20-YEARS AND WAS TRADED TO THE N.Y. METS (1972). AFTER 2-SEASONS...RETIRED. HE GAVE HIS VERY BEST FOR 22-YEARS. THE GREAT CENTER FIELDER WAS THE SECOND TO HIT 600 HOME RUNS...ON SEPT 21,1969. AARON CAUGHT HIM AT 648. FOR 15-YEARS (1954-68) HE HIT OVER 22 HOMERS AND AS MANY AS 52 (1965). OVER 3,000 HITS...FIRST TO STEAL 300 BASES... HE RE-WROTE THE RECORD BOOK. A SUPER-STAR... WHO IS A SURE BET TO ENTER THE **HALL** OF **FAME!**

WILLIE HIT 4 HOME RUNS IN ONE GAME. (MILW. BRAVES) APRIL 30, 1961

A FLAWLESS FIELDER. HIS GREAT CATCH OF VIC WERTZ'S TERRIFIC DRIVE...SAVED THE OPENING GAME OF THE 1954 WORLD SERIES FOR THE GIANTS VS CLEVELAND.

GEO LEE

© 1983 George L. Lee Feature Service

BASEBALL's HALL of FAMER

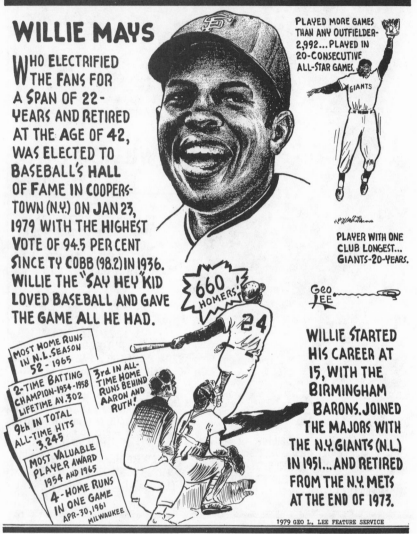

WILLIE MAYS

WHO ELECTRIFIED THE FANS FOR A SPAN OF 22-YEARS AND RETIRED AT THE AGE OF 42, WAS ELECTED TO BASEBALL'S HALL OF FAME IN COOPERS-TOWN (N.Y.) ON JAN 23, 1979 WITH THE HIGHEST VOTE OF 94.5 PER CENT SINCE TY COBB (98.2) IN 1936. WILLIE THE "SAY HEY"KID LOVED BASEBALL AND GAVE THE GAME ALL HE HAD.

PLAYED MORE GAMES THAN ANY OUTFIELDER- 2,992... PLAYED IN 20-CONSECUTIVE ALL-STAR GAMES.

PLAYER WITH ONE CLUB LONGEST... GIANTS-20-YEARS.

Geo LEE

660 HOMERS!

24

MOST HOME RUNS IN N.L. SEASON 52 - 1965

2-TIME BATTING CHAMPION-1954-1958 LIFETIME AV.302

3rd IN ALL-TIME HOME RUNS BEHIND AARON AND RUTH!

9th IN TOTAL ALL-TIME HITS 3,245

MOST VALUABLE PLAYER AWARD 1954 AND 1965

4-HOME RUNS IN ONE GAME APR-30,1961 MILWAUKEE

WILLIE STARTED HIS CAREER AT 15, WITH THE BIRMINGHAM BARONS. JOINED THE MAJORS WITH THE N.Y. GIANTS (N.L.) IN 1951... AND RETIRED FROM THE N.Y. METS AT THE END OF 1973.

1979 GEO L. LEE FEATURE SERVICE

JOE BLACK

VICE-PRESIDENT OF SPECIAL MARKETS...FOR GREYHOUND CORP., IN CHICAGO SINCE 1969 ON THE CORPORATE LEVEL. A NATIVE OF PLAINSFIELD, N.J., AND A GRADUATE OF MORGAN STATE COLLEGE WITH A B.S. IN PHYSICAL-EDUCATION AND PSYCHOLOGY. AN ALL-AROUND ATHLETE, HE TURNED TO BASE-BALL AND PLAYED AS PITCHER FOR THE BROOKLYN DODGERS IN EARLY

Geo Lee

JOE, THE ACE RELIEF PITCHER WAS THE FIRST BLACK TO WIN A WORLDS SERIES GAME IN 1952!

FIFTIES. IN 1952 WON "ROOKIE OF THE YEAR", AWARD OF THE NAT'L LEAGUE. BEFORE JOIN-ING GREYHOUND IN 1962 HE TAUGHT SCHOOL IN PLAINFIELD, AWARDED-HONORARY DOCTOR OF HUMANE LETTERS DEGREE BY SHAW COLLEGE AT DETROIT IN 1974.

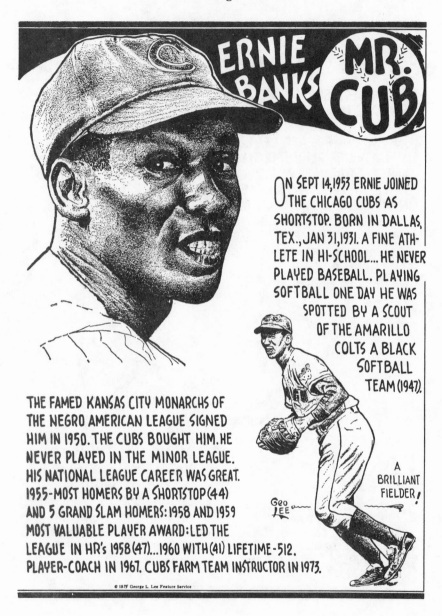

ERNIE BANKS
MR. CUB

ON SEPT 14,1953 ERNIE JOINED THE CHICAGO CUBS AS SHORTSTOP. BORN IN DALLAS, TEX., JAN 31,1931. A FINE ATH-LETE IN HI-SCHOOL... HE NEVER PLAYED BASEBALL. PLAYING SOFTBALL ONE DAY HE WAS SPOTTED BY A SCOUT OF THE AMARILLO COLTS A BLACK SOFTBALL TEAM (1947).

THE FAMED KANSAS CITY MONARCHS OF THE NEGRO AMERICAN LEAGUE SIGNED HIM IN 1950. THE CUBS BOUGHT HIM. HE NEVER PLAYED IN THE MINOR LEAGUE. HIS NATIONAL LEAGUE CAREER WAS GREAT. 1955-MOST HOMERS BY A SHORTSTOP (44) AND 5 GRAND SLAM HOMERS: 1958 AND 1959 MOST VALUABLE PLAYER AWARD: LED THE LEAGUE IN HR's 1958 (47)...1960 WITH (41) LIFETIME -512. PLAYER-COACH IN 1967. CUBS FARM TEAM INSTRUCTOR IN 1973.

A BRILLIANT FIELDER!

Geo LEE

SAM 'TOOTHPICK' JONES
1926-1971

FIRST BLACK TO PITCH A NO-HIT GAME! IN THE MAJORS

SOLID GOLD

ON MAY 12,1955 IN CHICAGO AT WRIGLEY FIELD... SAM PITCHING FOR THE CUBS... USED 136-PITCHES TO BEAT, PIRATES OF PITTSBURGH 4-0 AND GAIN HALL OF FAME HONORS...FOR A NO-HIT GAME! THE FIRST FOR CUBS IN 38-YEARS. THE 29-YEAR OLD PITCHER NEEDED ONLY 1-TOOTHPICK...FOR HIS BIG MOMENT IN BASEBALL'S HISTORY. HIS HABIT OF CHEWING ON TOOTH-PICKS GAVE HIM HIS 'NICKNAME'. HE WAS AWARDED A GOLD TOOTHPICK!

Geo LEE

GO-GO REMEMBER MINNIE?

ORESTES (MINNIE) MINOSO

STAR OUTFIELDER FOR THE CHICAGO WHITE SOX IN 1955 WAS NAMED CUBA'S No1 PRO-ATHLETE FOR THE THIRD TIME.

HERE I AM!

WHITE SOX

IN 1951 MINOSO JOINED THE SOX AND HIT .326. THE N.Y. CUBANS SOLD HIM TO THE CLEVELAND CLUB (1947). HE PLAYED ON THEIR SAN DIEGO TEAM BEFORE JOIN-ING THE INDIANS (1948)... MINNIE PLAYED 15-YEARS IN THE MAJORS...

MINNIE COME BACK

I'LL HIT WITH ONE HAND

Geo LEE

A POWER HITTER...BUT ALWAYS GETTING HIT WITH THE BALL. GAME AS THEY COME...IT WAS HARD TO KEEP HIM OUT OF THE LINE-UP. AT 48 HE WAS STILL PLAYING...MEXICO'S WINTER LEAGUE. (1969)

© 1975 George L. Lee Feature Service

94

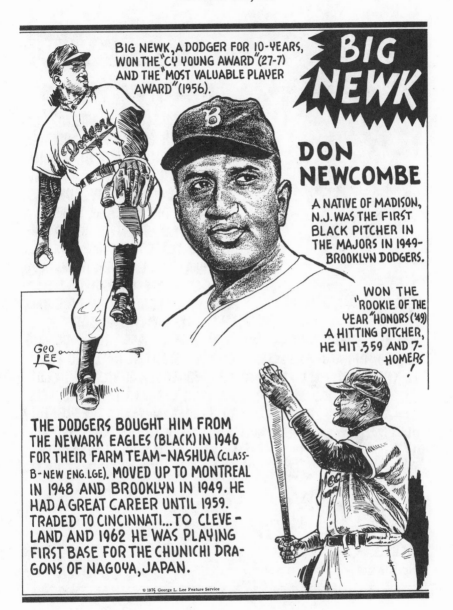

BIG NEWK, A DODGER FOR 10-YEARS, WON THE "CY YOUNG AWARD" (27-7) AND THE "MOST VALUABLE PLAYER AWARD" (1956).

BIG NEWK

DON NEWCOMBE

A NATIVE OF MADISON, N.J. WAS THE FIRST BLACK PITCHER IN THE MAJORS IN 1949- BROOKLYN DODGERS.

WON THE "ROOKIE OF THE YEAR" HONORS ('49) A HITTING PITCHER, HE HIT .359 AND 7- HOMERS!

Geo LEE

THE DODGERS BOUGHT HIM FROM THE NEWARK EAGLES (BLACK) IN 1946 FOR THEIR FARM TEAM - NASHUA (CLASS-B - NEW ENG. LGE). MOVED UP TO MONTREAL IN 1948 AND BROOKLYN IN 1949. HE HAD A GREAT CAREER UNTIL 1959. TRADED TO CINCINNATI... TO CLEVE - LAND AND 1962 HE WAS PLAYING FIRST BASE FOR THE CHUNICHI DRA- GONS OF NAGOYA, JAPAN.

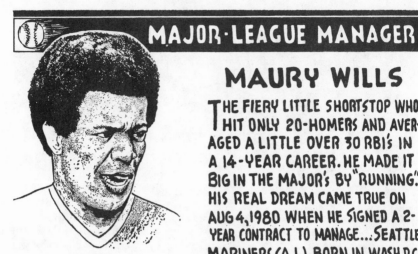

MAJOR·LEAGUE MANAGER

MAURY WILLS

THE FIERY LITTLE SHORTSTOP WHO HIT ONLY 20-HOMERS AND AVERAGED A LITTLE OVER 30 RBI'S IN A 14-YEAR CAREER. HE MADE IT BIG IN THE MAJOR'S BY "RUNNING." HIS REAL DREAM CAME TRUE ON AUG 4,1980 WHEN HE SIGNED A 2-YEAR CONTRACT TO MANAGE...SEATTLE MARINERS (A.L). BORN IN WASH,D.C, ON OCT 2,1932 THE SON OF A BAPTIST MINISTER. MAURY ORIGINALLY SIGNED WITH THE DODGERS IN 1951 AND SPENT 8-YEARS IN THE MINORS. IN 1959 THE L.A.DODGERS SIGNED HIM AND AN EXCITING CAREER STARTED. HE LEAD THEM TO THEIR FIRST N.L.PENNANT AND WORLD SERIES VICTORY IN LOS ANGELES. IN 1962 HE WON THE N.L'S MOST VALUABLE PLAYER AWARD. TRADED IN 1967 TO THE PIRATES THEN MONTREAL...BACK TO THE DODGERS (1969).

LIFETIME BATTING AV. 281!

STOLE 586 BASES!

SET A RECORD 104 BASES IN 1962! BEATING TY COBB'S 96 (1915)

MAURY PLAYED UNTIL 1972. BECAME AN INSTRUCTOR AND A TV BASEBALL BROADCASTER

Geo LEE

1980 GEO L. LEE FEATURE SERVICE

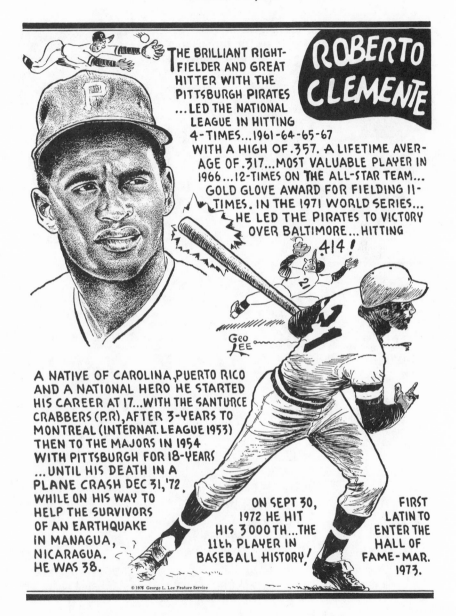

THE BRILLIANT RIGHT-FIELDER AND GREAT HITTER WITH THE PITTSBURGH PIRATES ...LED THE NATIONAL LEAGUE IN HITTING 4-TIMES...1961-64-65-67 WITH A HIGH OF .357. A LIFETIME AVERAGE OF .317...MOST VALUABLE PLAYER IN 1966...12-TIMES ON THE ALL-STAR TEAM... GOLD GLOVE AWARD FOR FIELDING 11-TIMES. IN THE 1971 WORLD SERIES... HE LED THE PIRATES TO VICTORY OVER BALTIMORE...HITTING .414!

ROBERTO CLEMENTE

A NATIVE OF CAROLINA, PUERTO RICO AND A NATIONAL HERO HE STARTED HIS CAREER AT 17...WITH THE SANTURCE CRABBERS (P.R), AFTER 3-YEARS TO MONTREAL (INTERNAT. LEAGUE 1953) THEN TO THE MAJORS IN 1954 WITH PITTSBURGH FOR 18-YEARS ...UNTIL HIS DEATH IN A PLANE CRASH DEC 31, '72 WHILE ON HIS WAY TO HELP THE SURVIVORS OF AN EARTHQUAKE IN MANAGUA, NICARAGUA. HE WAS 38.

ON SEPT 30, 1972 HE HIT HIS 3000TH...THE 11th PLAYER IN BASEBALL HISTORY!

FIRST LATIN TO ENTER THE HALL OF FAME- MAR. 1973.

GEO LEE

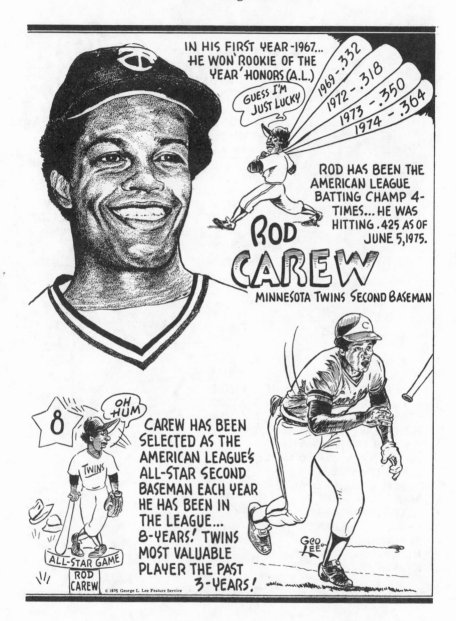

IN HIS FIRST YEAR -1967...
HE WON 'ROOKIE OF THE
YEAR' HONORS (A.L.)

GUESS I'M
JUST LUCKY

1969 - .332
1972 - .318
1973 - .350
1974 - .364

ROD HAS BEEN THE
AMERICAN LEAGUE
BATTING CHAMP 4-
TIMES... HE WAS
HITTING .425 AS OF
JUNE 5, 1975.

ROD
CAREW
MINNESOTA TWINS SECOND BASEMAN

OH HUM

8

TWINS

ALL-STAR GAME
ROD CAREW
© 1975 George L. Lee Feature Service

CAREW HAS BEEN
SELECTED AS THE
AMERICAN LEAGUE'S
ALL-STAR SECOND
BASEMAN EACH YEAR
HE HAS BEEN IN
THE LEAGUE...
8-YEARS! TWINS
MOST VALUABLE
PLAYER THE PAST
3-YEARS!

Geo Lee

98

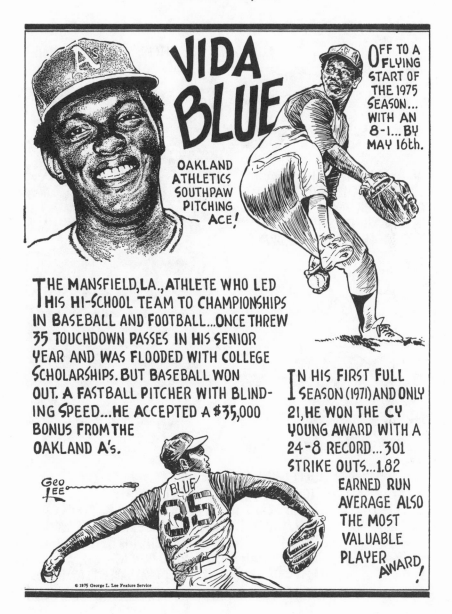

VIDA BLUE

OAKLAND ATHLETICS SOUTHPAW PITCHING ACE!

OFF TO A FLYING START OF THE 1975 SEASON... WITH AN 8-1... BY MAY 16th.

THE MANSFIELD, LA., ATHLETE WHO LED HIS HI-SCHOOL TEAM TO CHAMPIONSHIPS IN BASEBALL AND FOOTBALL...ONCE THREW 35 TOUCHDOWN PASSES IN HIS SENIOR YEAR AND WAS FLOODED WITH COLLEGE SCHOLARSHIPS. BUT BASEBALL WON OUT. A FASTBALL PITCHER WITH BLINDING SPEED...HE ACCEPTED A $35,000 BONUS FROM THE OAKLAND A's.

IN HIS FIRST FULL SEASON (1971) AND ONLY 21, HE WON THE CY YOUNG AWARD WITH A 24-8 RECORD...301 STRIKE OUTS...1.82 EARNED RUN AVERAGE ALSO THE MOST VALUABLE PLAYER AWARD!

Geo Lee

BLUE 35

99

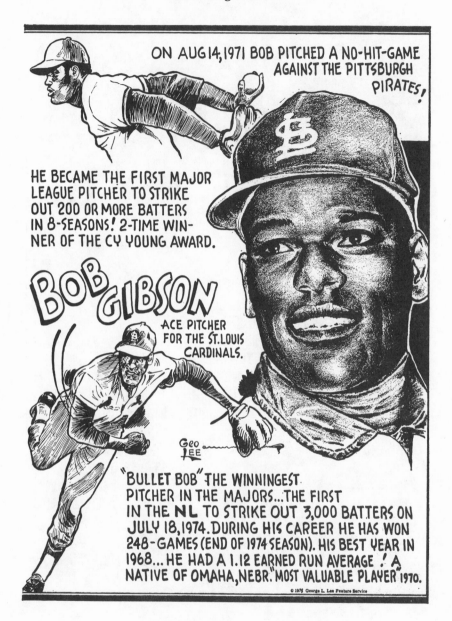

ON AUG 14, 1971 BOB PITCHED A NO-HIT-GAME AGAINST THE PITTSBURGH PIRATES!

HE BECAME THE FIRST MAJOR LEAGUE PITCHER TO STRIKE OUT 200 OR MORE BATTERS IN 8-SEASONS! 2-TIME WINNER OF THE CY YOUNG AWARD.

BOB GIBSON

ACE PITCHER FOR THE ST.LOUIS CARDINALS.

Geo Lee

"BULLET BOB" THE WINNINGEST PITCHER IN THE MAJORS...THE FIRST IN THE **NL** TO STRIKE OUT 3,000 BATTERS ON JULY 18, 1974. DURING HIS CAREER HE HAS WON 248-GAMES (END OF 1974 SEASON). HIS BEST YEAR IN 1968... HE HAD A 1.12 EARNED RUN AVERAGE! A NATIVE OF OMAHA, NEBR. "MOST VALUABLE PLAYER" 1970.

© 1975 George L. Lee Feature Service

100

WILLIE STARGELL
PITTSBURGH PIRATES LEFTFIELDER

WILLIE WON THE 1973 "ROBERTO CLEMENTE AWARD" GIVEN TO THE PLAYER WHO "BEST EXEMPLIFIES THE GAME OF BASEBALL ON AND OFF THE FIELD."

MISSED AGAIN!

MOST VALUABLE PLAYER

A NATIVE OF EARLSBORO, OKLA., WAS SIGNED BY THE PIRATES IN 1959 FOR ONLY $1,500. HE PLAYED HIS MINOR LEAGUE BALL IN TEXAS. IN 1971 HE LED THE PIRATES INTO THE WORLD SERIES WITH 48 HOMERS BUT MISSED THE MOST VALUABLE PLAYER AWARD AND AGAIN IN 1973. WILLIE CONTINUES HIS BIG KEY HITS TO KEEP THE PIRATES ON TOP IN THE EAST DIVISION. JULY '75

© 1975 George L. Lee Feature Service

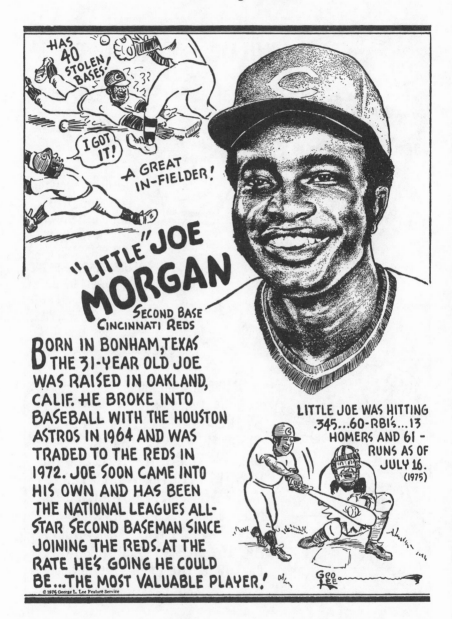

HAS 40 STOLEN BASES!

I GOT IT!

A GREAT IN-FIELDER!

"LITTLE" JOE MORGAN
SECOND BASE
CINCINNATI REDS

BORN IN BONHAM, TEXAS THE 31-YEAR OLD JOE WAS RAISED IN OAKLAND, CALIF. HE BROKE INTO BASEBALL WITH THE HOUSTON ASTROS IN 1964 AND WAS TRADED TO THE REDS IN 1972. JOE SOON CAME INTO HIS OWN AND HAS BEEN THE NATIONAL LEAGUES ALL-STAR SECOND BASEMAN SINCE JOINING THE REDS. AT THE RATE HE'S GOING HE COULD BE... THE MOST VALUABLE PLAYER!

© 1975 George L. Lee Feature Service

LITTLE JOE WAS HITTING .345...60-RBI's...13 HOMERS AND 61 - RUNS AS OF JULY 16. (1975)

Geo Lee

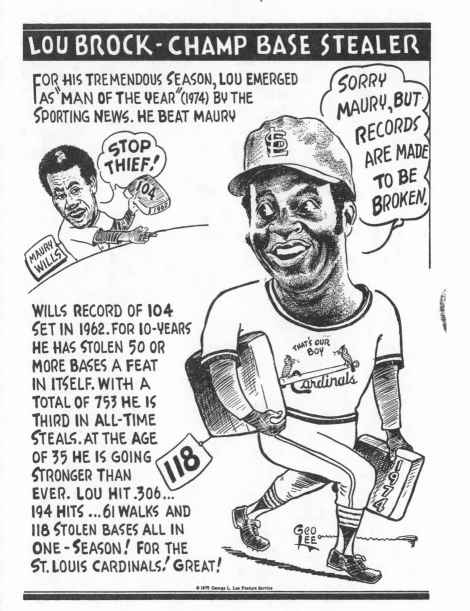

LOU BROCK - CHAMP BASE STEALER

FOR HIS TREMENDOUS SEASON, LOU EMERGED AS "MAN OF THE YEAR" (1974) BY THE SPORTING NEWS. HE BEAT MAURY

WILLS RECORD OF 104 SET IN 1962. FOR 10-YEARS HE HAS STOLEN 50 OR MORE BASES A FEAT IN ITSELF. WITH A TOTAL OF 753 HE IS THIRD IN ALL-TIME STEALS. AT THE AGE OF 35 HE IS GOING STRONGER THAN EVER. LOU HIT .306... 194 HITS ... 61 WALKS AND 118 STOLEN BASES ALL IN ONE - SEASON! FOR THE ST. LOUIS CARDINALS! GREAT!

© 1975 George L. Lee Feature Service

LU-*IS!* LU-*IS!* LU-*IS!*

THE EVER POPULAR BOSTON ACE PITCHER WHOSE EFFORTS LED THEM INTO THE PLAY-OFFS AND THEN INTO THE WORLD SERIES WITH CINCINNATI. HIS FIRST. LUIS WON 2-SERIES GAMES BUT BOSTON LOST AND THE CINCY REDS...THE 1975 CHAMPS!

LUIS TIANT

CUBAN PITCHER FOR THE BOSTON RED SOX WHO HAS AMAZING CONTROL.

Geo
LEE

THE SON OF ONE OF CUBA'S ALL-TIME GREAT PITCHERS, LUIS STARTED HIS CAREER AT 17 IN MEXICO. WENT TO CLEVELAND IN 1964 AND WITH THEM LED THE (AL) LEAGUE IN 1968 WITH 21-9 AND A 1.60 ERA. AFTER A SLUMP TRADED TO THE MINN.,TWINS (1970). BOSTON SIGNED HIM FOR THEIR FARM CLUB (1971) AND

BOSTON TOOK HIM THE SAME YEAR. AFTER A DISMAL SHOWING HE CAME THRU BIG IN 1972 TO LEAD THE LEAGUE WITH A 15-6 AND A 1.91 EARNED RUN AVER.

© 1975 George L. Lee Feature Service

105

FERGIE JENKINS

20-GAME WINNER 6-SEASONS!

BOSTON RED SOX PITCHER (A.L.) (1975), STARTED HIS MAJOR LEAGUE CAREER WITH THE NAT'L LEAGUE'S PHILLIES IN 1962. JOINED THE CHICAGO CUBS IN 1966. PITCHED HIS FIRST 20-GAME SEASON IN 1967 AND KEPT GOING UNTIL HE HAD 6-STRAIGHT 20-GAME SEASONS. WON THE NAT'L LEAGUE "CY YOUNG" AWARD IN 1971. CANADA'S "OUTSTANDING MALE ATHLETE" ('67-'68-'71). A NATIVE OF CHATHAM, ONTARIO, FERGIE WAS AN-AROUND ATHLETE IN VOCATIONAL HI-SCHOOL PLAYING HOCKEY, BASKETBALL AND BASEBALL!

FIRST

GENE BAKER,

A FORMER SECOND BASEMAN OF THE PITTSBURGH PIRATES IS THE FIRST BLACK MAJOR LEAGUER TO BECOME A MANAGER OF A FARM TEAM. IN 1962 HE WAS APPOINTED TO THE PIRATES' CLASS D, BATAVIA (N.Y.) CLUB OF THE N.Y.-PENNA LEAGUE. A NATIVE OF IOWA HE WAS THE FIRST BLACK TO INTEGRATE THE CHICAGO CUBS IN 1953. GENE WAS PICKED AS A SHORTSTOP FROM THE L.A. ANGELS OF THE PACIFIC COAST LEAGUE, A CUB FARM TEAM. ERNIE BANKS WAS SIGNED NEXT AS SHORTSTOP AND GENE MOVED TO SECOND MAKING A GREAT KEYSTONE DUO!

FRANK ROBINSON

OUTFIELDER FOR THE CALIF-ORNIA ANGELS IS THE ONLY PLAYER EVER TO WIN THE MOST VALUABLE PLAYER HONOR IN BOTH LEAGUES. NATIONAL:.IN 1961 WITH CINCINNATI REDS: AMERICAN ...IN 1966 WITH BALTIMORE ORIOLES!

Geo LEE.

JACKIE ROBINSON

FIRST BLACK IN ORGANIZED BASEBALL WON TOP HONORS IN HIS FIRST YEAR..1946..WITH THE MONTREAL ROYALS.

HIT .349   155! HITS!
65 RBI's   25 DOUBLES
8 TRIPLES 3 HOMERS

INTERNATIONAL LEAGUE
1946 BATTING CHAMPIONSHIP

STOLE 40 BASES

133 RUNS

'SATCHEL' PAIGE

PITCHING WITH THE K.C. MONARCH'S IN 1934..HE ONCE HURLED A NO-HIT GAME AGAINST THE HOMESTEAD GRAYS IN WASH. D.C..THEN RODE A 1,000 MI. BY AUTO TO BEAT THE CHICAGO AMERICAN GIANTS 1-0..12-INNINGS.

© 1974 George L. Lee Feature Service

107

Football
Players

ALL-TIME, ALL-AMERICAN GREAT

JUDGE FRED "DUKE" SLATER

1898 1966

RECEIVED HIS LAW DEGREE FROM IOWA U., IN 1928 AND STARTED HIS LEGAL CAREER IN 1935 IN CHICAGO AS ASS'T CITY CORP. COUNSEL. HE ROSE TO JUDGESHIP IN 1948 WHEN HE WAS ELECTED TO THE MUNICIPAL COURT; SUPERIOR COURT (1960); THE CIRCUIT COURT (1964). BORN IN NORMAL, ILL., WENT TO HI-SCHOOL IN CLINTON, IOWA. SON OF A MINISTER, HE PLAYED FOOTBALL. IN 1913 HELPED CLINTON HI WIN THE STATE TITLE.

PLAYING WITH IOWA "DUKE" NEVER WORE A HELMET!

GEO LEE

WENT TO IOWA U AND PLAYED TACKLE (1918-21), ALL-AMERICAN (1921). WON BIG "10" AND NAT'L TITLE IN 1921. PLAYED PRO-BALL (1922-32) WITH ROCK ISLAND (ILL) AND CHICAGO CARDINALS. DUKE WAS ALL-PRO IN '26 AND '31. IN 1946 600 SPORTS WRITERS NAMED HIM "ALL-TIME, ALL-AMERICAN TACKLE"

ENTERED INTO THE NATIONAL FOOTBALL LEAGUE-HALL OF FAME! 1951

© 1978 George L. Lee Feature Service

Chicago Defender   September 29, 1934

Chicago Defender   May 17, 1934

Chicago Defender   October 13, 1934

Chicago Defender   December 1, 1934

Chicago Defender   December 8, 1934

Chicago Defender   December 22, 1934

Chicago Defender   April 6, 1935

THE GREAT HALFBACK OF U.C.L.A...ONCE THREW A PASS 65-YD's AGAINST USC IN 1937 FOR A COLLEGIATE RECORD. A GREAT PASSER AND RUSHER...HE MADE THE ALL-AMERICAN TEAM IN 1939. HE JOINED THE HOLLYWOOD BEARS OF THE PACIFIC COAST PRO-LEAGUE IN 1940 AND WAS 4-TIMES ALL-PACIFIC HALFBACK.

KENNY WASHINGTON
1919-1971

WHO BROKE THE 13-YEAR COLOR-LINE OF THE NATIONAL FOOTBALL LEAGUE...WHEN HE SIGNED WITH THE L.A. RAMS IN 1946. HE WAS GREAT!

Geo LEE

HIS LAST SEASON...DUE TO INJURIES ...1949. HE OPENED THE DOOR FOR BLACKS IN PRO-FOOTBALL. BORN IN LOS ANGELES HE STARTED HIS ATHLETIC CAREER AT LINCOLN HI...PLAYING FOOTBALL, BASEBALL AND TRACK. KNOWN AS THE "GENERAL" AT UCLA...HE CALLED THE SIGNALS. IN 1955 VOTED ONE OF 2-GREATEST FOOTBALL PLAYERS OF ALL-TIME IN LOS ANGELES BY THE HELMS ATHLETIC FOUNDATION.

AT UCLA HE SET A RECORD OF 1915 YARDS RUSHING -1300 PASSING.

© 1975 George L. Lee Feature Service

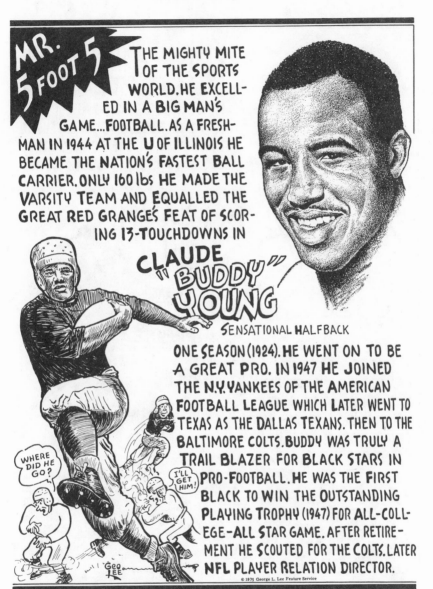

MR. 5 FOOT 5

THE MIGHTY MITE OF THE SPORTS WORLD. HE EXCELLED IN A BIG MAN'S GAME... FOOTBALL. AS A FRESHMAN IN 1944 AT THE U OF ILLINOIS HE BECAME THE NATION'S FASTEST BALL CARRIER. ONLY 160 lbs HE MADE THE VARSITY TEAM AND EQUALLED THE GREAT RED GRANGE'S FEAT OF SCORING 13-TOUCHDOWNS IN

CLAUDE "BUDDY" YOUNG

SENSATIONAL HALFBACK

WHERE DID HE GO?

I'LL GET HIM!

ONE SEASON (1924). HE WENT ON TO BE A GREAT PRO. IN 1947 HE JOINED THE N.Y. YANKEES OF THE AMERICAN FOOTBALL LEAGUE WHICH LATER WENT TO TEXAS AS THE DALLAS TEXANS. THEN TO THE BALTIMORE COLTS. BUDDY WAS TRULY A TRAIL BLAZER FOR BLACK STARS IN PRO-FOOTBALL. HE WAS THE FIRST BLACK TO WIN THE OUTSTANDING PLAYING TROPHY (1947) FOR ALL-COLLEGE-ALL STAR GAME. AFTER RETIREMENT HE SCOUTED FOR THE COLTS. LATER NFL PLAYER RELATION DIRECTOR.

Geo Lee

© 1975 George L. Lee Feature Service

119

FOOTBALL'S HALL OF FAMER AND ALL-TIME NFL PRO STARTED HIS GREAT CAREER IN 1948. IN COLLEGE HE WAS OUTSTANDING AT U OF IOWA AND U OF TOLEDO AS AN OFFENSIVE BACK ALSO IN THE COAST GUARD. EM WAS THE FIRST BLACK SIGNED

EMLEN TUNNELL

THE GREAT DEFENSIVE HALFBACK OF THE N.Y. GIANTS (1948-58) AND THE GREEN BAY PACKERS (1959-61)

BY THE N.Y. GIANTS. A NATIVE OF GARRETT HILL, PA., HE LEFT IOWA TO PLAY WITH THE GIANTS. AFTER HIS PLAYING DAYS HE BECAME A COACH AND A SCOUT FOR THE GIANTS.

HEY

SIGN RIGHT NOW

MOST INTERCEPTIONS BY CAREER— 79!

MOST PUNT RETURNS —CAREER 258 FOR 2,209 YDS!

© 1975 George L. Lee Feature Service

120

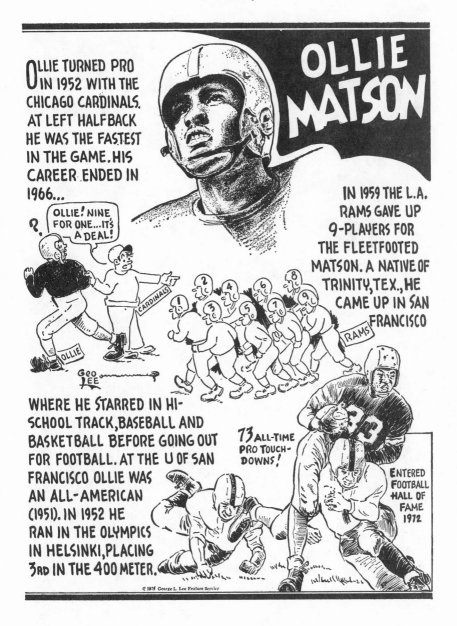

OLLIE MATSON

OLLIE TURNED PRO IN 1952 WITH THE CHICAGO CARDINALS. AT LEFT HALFBACK HE WAS THE FASTEST IN THE GAME. HIS CAREER ENDED IN 1966...

OLLIE! NINE FOR ONE...IT'S A DEAL!

IN 1959 THE L.A. RAMS GAVE UP 9-PLAYERS FOR THE FLEETFOOTED MATSON. A NATIVE OF TRINITY, TEX., HE CAME UP IN SAN FRANCISCO

WHERE HE STARRED IN HI-SCHOOL TRACK, BASEBALL AND BASKETBALL BEFORE GOING OUT FOR FOOTBALL. AT THE U OF SAN FRANCISCO OLLIE WAS AN ALL-AMERICAN (1951). IN 1952 HE RAN IN THE OLYMPICS IN HELSINKI, PLACING 3RD IN THE 400 METER.

73 ALL-TIME PRO TOUCH-DOWNS!

ENTERED FOOTBALL HALL OF FAME 1972

Geo Lee

© 1979 George L. Lee Feature Service

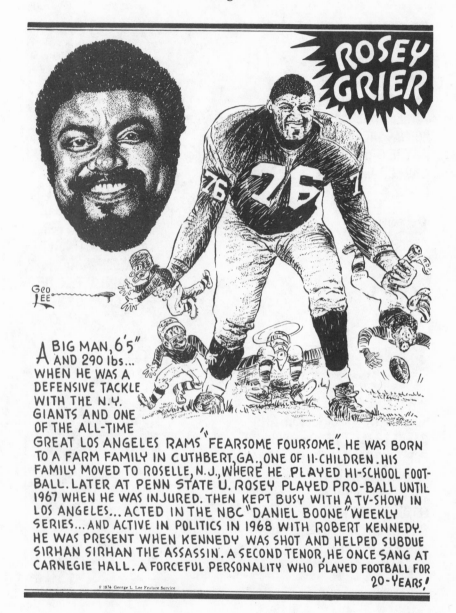

ROSEY GRIER

Geo
Lee

A BIG MAN, 6'5"
AND 290 lbs...
WHEN HE WAS A
DEFENSIVE TACKLE
WITH THE N.Y.
GIANTS AND ONE
OF THE ALL-TIME
GREAT LOS ANGELES RAMS "FEARSOME FOURSOME". HE WAS BORN
TO A FARM FAMILY IN CUTHBERT, GA., ONE OF 11-CHILDREN. HIS
FAMILY MOVED TO ROSELLE, N.J., WHERE HE PLAYED HI-SCHOOL FOOT-
BALL. LATER AT PENN STATE U. ROSEY PLAYED PRO-BALL UNTIL
1967 WHEN HE WAS INJURED. THEN KEPT BUSY WITH A TV-SHOW IN
LOS ANGELES... ACTED IN THE NBC "DANIEL BOONE" WEEKLY
SERIES... AND ACTIVE IN POLITICS IN 1968 WITH ROBERT KENNEDY.
HE WAS PRESENT WHEN KENNEDY WAS SHOT AND HELPED SUBDUE
SIRHAN SIRHAN THE ASSASSIN. A SECOND TENOR, HE ONCE SANG AT
CARNEGIE HALL. A FORCEFUL PERSONALITY WHO PLAYED FOOTBALL FOR
20-YEARS!

FOOTBALL · ART · POET · ACTOR

BERNIE CASEY

HIGHLY TALENTED ATHLETE, AN ACCOMPLISHED ARTIST, A PUBLISHED POET AND A FINE ACTOR. BORN IN WYCO, W. VA., IN 1939 AND GREW UP IN COLUMBUS, OHIO. STUDIED AT EAST HIGH, PLAYED SPORTS AND WANTED TO BE AN ARTIST. HE WON AN ATHLETIC SCHOLARSHIP TO BOWLING GREEN STATE U., PLAYED FOOTBALL AND STUDIED PAINTING. IN 1961 HE JOINED PRO-FOOTBALL WITH THE SAN FRANCISCO 49'ERS AS A FLANKER-BACK. BERNIE HAD HIS FIRST ONE-MAN

Geo LEE

ART SHOW (1963), IN FRISCO. BY STUDYING OFF-SEASON HE EARNED HIS MASTER'S IN FINE ARTS IN 1966. (BOWLING GREEN). MOVING TO THE L. A. RAMS, HE STUDIED ACTING AT THE JEFF COREY ACTING SCHOOL ONE OF THE FINEST. BERNIE RETIRED FROM FOOTBALL IN 1969 AND BEGAN HIS ACTING CAREER IN "GUNS OF THE MAGNIFICENT SEVEN." FIRST BOOK OF POETRY "LOOK AT THE PEOPLE." HIS PAINTINGS IN THE PRIVATE COLLECTION OF J. HIRSHHORN THE BEST.

6'4" AND OVER 200 lbs. ALL-AMERICAN HALFBACK AT BOWLING GREEN. LED 49'ERS IN PASSES CAUGHT AND YDS GAINED, FOR 3-YEARS. STARRED FOR THE RAMS. ONE OF NFL'S TOP RECEIVERS.

1979 GEO L. LEE FEATURE SERVICE

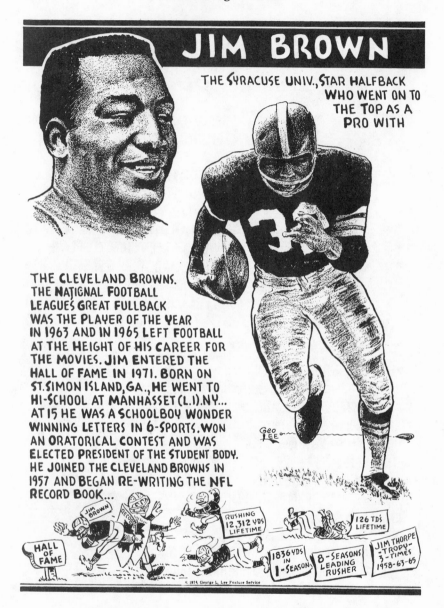

JIM BROWN

THE SYRACUSE UNIV., STAR HALFBACK WHO WENT ON TO THE TOP AS A PRO WITH

THE CLEVELAND BROWNS. THE NATIONAL FOOTBALL LEAGUES GREAT FULLBACK WAS THE PLAYER OF THE YEAR IN 1963 AND IN 1965 LEFT FOOTBALL AT THE HEIGHT OF HIS CAREER FOR THE MOVIES. JIM ENTERED THE HALL OF FAME IN 1971. BORN ON ST. SIMON ISLAND, GA., HE WENT TO HI-SCHOOL AT MANHASSET (L.I). NY... AT 15 HE WAS A SCHOOLBOY WONDER WINNING LETTERS IN 6-SPORTS. WON AN ORATORICAL CONTEST AND WAS ELECTED PRESIDENT OF THE STUDENT BODY. HE JOINED THE CLEVELAND BROWNS IN 1957 AND BEGAN RE-WRITING THE NFL RECORD BOOK...

GEO LEE

JIM BROWN

HALL OF FAME

RUSHING 12,312 YDS LIFETIME

1836 YDS IN 1-SEASON

8-SEASONS LEADING RUSHER

126 TD'S LIFETIME

JIM THORPE -TROPY- 3-TIMES 1958-63-65

© 1974 George L. Lee Feature Service

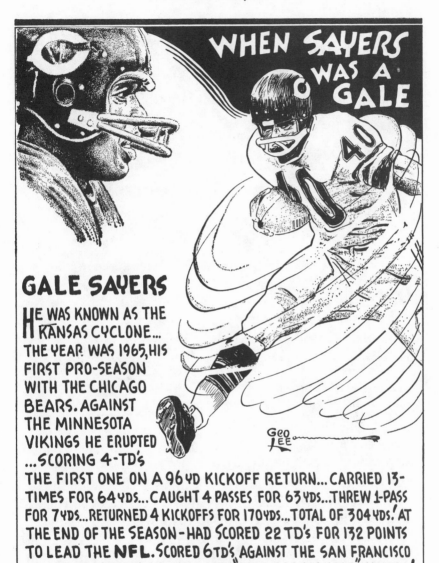

WHEN SAYERS WAS A GALE

GALE SAYERS

He WAS KNOWN AS THE KANSAS CYCLONE... THE YEAR WAS 1965, HIS FIRST PRO-SEASON WITH THE CHICAGO BEARS. AGAINST THE MINNESOTA VIKINGS HE ERUPTED ...SCORING 4-TD's THE FIRST ONE ON A 96 YD KICKOFF RETURN... CARRIED 13-TIMES FOR 64 YDS... CAUGHT 4 PASSES FOR 63 YDS... THREW 1-PASS FOR 7 YDS... RETURNED 4 KICKOFFS FOR 170 YDS... TOTAL OF 304 YDS! AT THE END OF THE SEASON - HAD SCORED 22 TD's FOR 132 POINTS TO LEAD THE **NFL**. SCORED 6 TD's AGAINST THE SAN FRANCISCO 49ERS. THE KANSAS CYCLONE WON "ROOKIE OF THE YEAR" HONORS!

GEO LEE

© 1979 George L. Lee Feature Service

O.J. SIMPSON
BUFFALO BILLS RUNNING BACK

WHO WON THE 1968 HEISMAN TROPHY PLAYED TWO SEASONS FOR USC. HE WAS THE FIRST TO GAIN 3,000-YDS IN 2-SEASONS IN COLLEGE FOOTBALL... THE TOP GRID STAR OF THE 1960's. O.J., STARTED HIS GREAT CAREER AT GALILEO HI-SCHOOL IN SAN FRANCISCO MAKING ALL-CITY FULLBACK. THEN...SAN FRANCISCO CITY COLLEGE AS FLANKER-BACK SCORING 54-TD's... ON TO USC TO RE-WRITE THE RECORD BOOK. IN 1969 HE WAS DRAFTED BY THE BUFFALO BILLS OF THE AFL. IN 1973 HE REALLY MADE IT BIG IN THE PROS...THE FIRST TO GAIN OVER 2,000-YDS IN ONE SEASON! HALL OF FAME-"HERE I COME."

CAN HE DO IT AGAIN ?

ARCHIE GRIFFIN

Geo LEE

OHIO STATE'S GREAT RUNNING BACK WHO WON THE 1974 HEISMAN TROPHY GIVEN TO THE TOP COLLEGE-FOOTBALL PLAYER IN THE U.S. HE IS THE 5th JUNIOR TO WIN THE AWARD. A REPEAT OF LAST YEARS PERFORMANCE COULD DO IT AGAIN. SO FAR NO ONE HAS WON TWICE. ONLY 5 FT 9, 185 POUNDS OF RAW SPEED HE GAINED 100 YARDS OR MORE IN 22 STRAIGHT GAMES. ARCHIE MADE 239-YARDS IN HIS FIRST COLLEGE GAME AGAINST NORTH CAROLINA (1972).

© 1975 George L. Lee Feature Service

Basketball
Players

Chicago Defender   October 27, 1934

BORN IN MONROE, LA., HE STARTED HIS GREAT BASKETBALL CAREER IN THE SMALL JESUIT SCHOOL, THE U OF SAN FRANCISCO - NICKNAMED THE...DONS. BILL A 6'10" CENTER WITH A 7-FOOT SPAN SOON BE-CAME AN ALL-AMERICAN AND POWERED THE DONS TO A 60-GAME WIN STREAK AND 2-NCAA TITLES. IN 1956 HE LED THE U.S.OLYMPIC TEAM TO A GOLD MEDAL. THE BOSTON CELTICS OF THE NBA SIGNED HIM AND FOR 13-YEARS LED THEM TO 11-CHAMPION-SHIPS. IN 1966 HE BECAME THE CELTICS COACH-PLAYER THE FIRST BLACK IN THE NBA. BILL RETIRED IN 1969. IN 1973 HE SIGNED AS COACH-GEN.MANAGER OF THE SEATTLE SUPERSONICS.

SORRY BILL YOUR JEST NOT GOOD ENUFF!

AW COACH

- ONCE CUT FROM THE FIRST TEAM SQUAD AFTER PLAYING RESERVE ON THE SQUAD FOR A-YEAR AT McCLYMONDS HIGH IN OAKLAND, CALIF....A BITTER DISAPPOINTMENT.

ONE OF THE GREATEST DEFENSIVE PLAYERS IN ALL BASKETBALL.. 5 TIMES-MOST VALUABLE PLAYER!

Geo LEE

© 1974 George L. Lee Feature Service

ELGIN BAYLOR

WOW! LOOK AT THAT BODY CONTROL!

THE GREAT ALL-AROUND SUPERSTAR OF THE LOS ANGELES LAKERS. DURING HIS CAREER HE SCORED 23,149 POINTS-11,463 REBOUNDS ...SCORED 2,719 IN 1-SEASON ('62-'63) AVERAGING 38.2 POINTS PER GAME!

HE PLAYED FOR 13-YEARS AND WAS CAPTAIN FOR 12...ALL-PRO 11-YEARS. A NATIVE OF WASH.D.C., HE WAS ALL-CITY AND ALL-METRO AT SPINGARN HI-SCHOOL. AT SEATTLE U.,HE WAS AN ALL-AMERICAN TWICE. THE SLUMPING MINNEA-POLIS LAKERS SIGNED HIM IN 1958 AND HIS GREAT ABILITY SPARKED THEM TO THE TOP. MOVING TO L.A. THEY BECAME THE LOS ANGELES LAKERS. A GREAT BLACK ATHLETE!

GEO LEE

ELGIN ONCE SCORED 71-PTS AGAINST THE N.Y. KNICKS (1960) HE RETIRED-1971.

KAREEM ABDUL-JABBAR

CAN HE TURN THE LOS ANGELES LAKERS AROUND LIKE HE DID THE MILWAUKEE BUCKS?

THE 7'2" TOWERING OFFENSIVE STAR HAS A 7'5" ARMS SPAN FOR DEFENSE!

Geo LEE

KAREEM TOOK THE BUCKS FROM A 27-55 LOSER TO A 56-26 WINNER IN HIS FIRST SEASON (1969). THE LAKERS FINISHED LAST IN THE WESTERN CONFERENCE (30-52) IN 1974-75. THE GREAT **UCLA** STAR WHO MADE BASKETBALL HISTORY... STARTED HIS TREMENDOUS CAREER AT NYC's POWER MEMORIAL ACADEMY (HI-SCHOOL). HE LED THEM TO 71-STRAIGHT WINS AND DURING HIS LAST 3-YEARS THE TEAM ONLY LOST ONE GAME. JABBAR SIGNED A MILLION PLUS CONTRACT WHEN HE JOINED THE BUCKS. NOW WITH THE LAKERS (1975)... ALL EYES WILL BE ON THE **BIG MAN!**

AL ATTLES – COACH OF THE GOLDEN STATE WARRIORS WHO LED HIS NBA TEAM TO THE TITLE IN THE 1974-75 SEASON BY BEATING THE WASHINGTON CAPITOL BULLETS IN 4-STRAIGHT GAMES.

THE BENCH

HIS GAME PLAN... 12-MAN TEAM...12-MEN PLAY. SO FAR IT HAS BEEN VERY SUCCESSFUL!

KNOWN AS "THE DESTROYER" DURING HIS PLAYING DAYS WITH THE WARRIORS... 11-YEARS. A NATIVE OF NEWARK, N.J., ATTLES PLAYED WITH HIS ALMA MATER, NORTH CAROLINA A&T BEFORE HE JOINED THE WARRIORS (PA). HE BECAME COACH IN 1970.

MIGHTY BOB M^cADOO

VOTED THE NATIONAL BASKETBALL ASSN'S MOST VALUABLE PLAYER LAST SEASON (1974-75) AND HIS SECOND STRAIGHT NBA SCORING CHAMPIONSHIP. THE BUFFALO BRAVES STAR CENTER SCORED 2,831 POINTS FOR AN AVERAGE OF 34.5 PER GAME... SECOND TO THE GREAT WILT CHAMBERLAIN. HE LED THE ASSOCIATION WITH 3,539 MINUTES PLAYED AND RANKED AMONG THE LEADERS IN FIELD GOAL PERCENTAGE, REBOUNDING AND BLOCKED SHOTS. BOB CAN DO IT ALL. THE NORTH CAROLINA STAR IS STARTING HIS 4TH-YEAR AS A PRO (1975). THE 6-10 CENTER JUST COULD BECOME THE GAMES GREATEST SHOOTER.

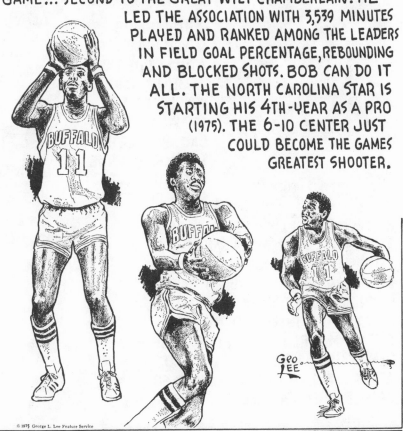

135

"LUSIA LUCY" HARRIS

SCORED 47-POINTS FOR DELTA WHEN THEY BEAT QUEENS COLLEGE IN MADISON SQ. GARDEN (1976)

OUTSTANDING WOMAN COLLEGE ATHLETE OF THE YEAR (1977) AND.... CONSIDERED THE TOP WOMAN BASKET-BALL PLAYER IN THE U.S...PLAYING WITH THE DELTA STATE UNIVERSITY (CLEVELAND, MISS.), LUCY LED THEM TO 3-STATE TITLES; 2-REGIONAL AND 2-NAT'L TITLES ALSO A MEMBER OF THE PAN-AMERICAN AND THE SILVER MEDAL WINNING WOMEN'S OLYMPIC TEAM (1976). A NATIVE OF MINTER CITY, MISS., THE 6'3" FARM GIRL IS THE 7th OF 9-CHILD-REN. SOUGHT AFTER BY DELTA STATE AFTER A FINE HI-SCHOOL CAREER, SHE GAINED NATIONAL RECOGNITION FOR DELTA!

Geo LEE

© 1978 George L. Lee Feature Service

Other Sports Figures

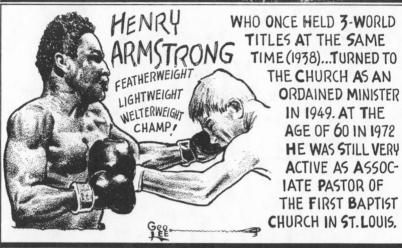

HENRY ARMSTRONG

FEATHERWEIGHT
LIGHTWEIGHT
WELTERWEIGHT
CHAMP!

WHO ONCE HELD 3-WORLD TITLES AT THE SAME TIME (1938)...TURNED TO THE CHURCH AS AN ORDAINED MINISTER IN 1949. AT THE AGE OF 60 IN 1972 HE WAS STILL VERY ACTIVE AS ASSOC-IATE PASTOR OF THE FIRST BAPTIST CHURCH IN ST. LOUIS.

JESSE OWENS

AT ANN ARBOR, MICH.

WOW! 26'8¼" WHATTA JUMP

ALL-TIME GREAT TRACK ATHLETE...HAD A BIG DAY-MAY 25, 1935-HE SET 3-NEW WORLD RECORDS: 220 YD-DASH 20.3, 220 YD-HURDLES 22.6 BROAD JUMP 26'8¼" AND EQUALLED THE 100 YD-DASH 9.4!

JACKIE ROBINSON

FIRST BLACK TO PLAY BASEBALL IN THE MAJOR LEAGUES WAS THE FIRST BLACK TO BE ELECT-ED TO THE BASEBALL HALL OF FAME AT COOPERSTOWN, N.Y., JAN 22, 1962.

MAURY WILLS
SHORTSTOP

IN 1962 WHILE PLAYING WITH THE LOS ANGELES DODGERS...HE STOLE 80 BASES TO BREAK THE 51-YEAR OLD NATIONAL LEAGUE RECORD AND BEAT THE GREAT TY COBB'S 47-YEAR RECORD OF 96 BASES IN 156 GAMES WITH 97! THEN STOLE 104 IN 162 GAMES... FOR A NEW RECORD!

BOBBY DOBBS
1858-1930

ONE OF THE MOST AMAZING BOXERS IN RING ANNALS. BORN IN KNOXVILLE, TENN., HIS CAREER BEGAN IN 1875 IN THE LIGHTWEIGHT CLASS. HE WAS 39 WHEN HE BEAT THE GREAT JOE GANS IN 20-RDS. ALTHO NEVER A WORLD CHAMP HE HAD A FANTASTIC CAREER FOR 40-YEARS. RING HISTORIANS CLAIM HE HAD 1000 FIGHTS...DOBBS WON LAST FIGHT IN 1915 ...AT THE AGE OF 57!

Geo. Lee

MARSHALL W. "MAJOR" TAYLOR
1878 - 1932

ONCE KNOWN AS "KING OF THE CYCLISTS"...HE WON THE WORLD CYCLE RACING CHAMPIONSHIP IN 1899 AND THE U.S. TITLE IN 1900... IN 1901 HE WENT TO EUROPE AND MET ALL-COMERS AND DEFEATED THEM. "THE FASTEST BIKE RIDER IN THE WORLD"... DURING HIS TIME!

SPORTIN' A-ROUND

DeHART HUBBARD

THE U OF MICHIGAN OLYMPIC BROAD 26'2" JUMP CHAMPION IN 1924 IN PARIS. HE MADE THE FIRST 26 FT JUMP IN 1928 BUT IT WAS DISALLOWED BECAUSE OF A MINOR PIT FLAW...31-YEARS LATER HE RECEIVED HIS RECOGNITION AWARD IN 1959!

OH BOY!

IT, DON'T COUNT

TIGER FLOWERS

OH YEAH

THAT'S IT

WON THE WORLD'S MIDDLE-WEIGHT TITLE FROM HARRY GREB ON FEB 26, 1926 AFTER HE HAD BEEN FLOORED 8-TIMES.

WILMA RUDOLPH

ENTERED THE NATIONAL HALL OF FAME FOR TRACK AND FIELD IN CHARLESTON, W.VA., IN 1974. THE GREAT TENNESSEE STATE U., STAR WON 3-GOLD MEDALS AT THE 1960 OLYMPICS IN ROME...THE 100-METER ...200 METER DASH AND ANCHORED THE WINNING RELAY TEAM.

Geo LEE

© 1976 George L. Lee Feature Service

ISAAC MURPHY

1859-1896

FIRST TO WIN
3-KENTUCKY DERBIES

THE GREATEST JOCKEY OF THE 19th CENTURY WAS BORN IN THE BLUE GRASS COUNTRY, AT WOODFORD CTY, KY. HE WAS 14 WHEN HE RODE HIS FIRST MOUNT. A YEAR LATER HE WON HIS FIRST RACE. AT 16 HE RODE SPRING BRANCH TO VICTORY IN THE BLUE GRASS

Geo LEE

STAKES AT CHURCH-HILL DOWNS IN 1875 ...AND UNTIL 1891 WAS WITHOUT A PEER IN THE RACING WORLD. DURING HIS CAREER HE RODE 1,412 MOUNTS WINNING 628 AN AVERAGE OF 44% WINNERS. HE RODE MODESTY A FILLY TO VICTORY IN THE FIRST AMERICAN DERBY IN 1884.

WASHINGTON PARK-CHICAGO

4-AMERICAN DERBIES

5-LATONIA DERBIES

© 1974, George L. Lee Feature Service

141

SHOW HORSE TRAINER

TOM BASS
1859 – 1934

BORN A SLAVE IN BOONE COUNTY, MO., THE PROPERTY OF A VERY WEALTHY SLAVE OWNER NAMED BASS. THE BASS STABLES WERE WELL-KNOWN AND YOUNG TOM WAS ALLOWED TO WORK IN THE STABLES. WITH HIS FREEDOM HE WORKED

AS A HOTEL BELL-BOY BUT HIS LOVE OF HORSES SOON FOUND HIM BACK WORK-ING THE STABLES. HIS ABILITY TO TRAIN AND RIDE SHOW HORSES WAS RECOGNIZED BY OWNERS EVERYWHERE. HE MADE MEXICO, MO., THE "SADDLE HORSE CAPITAL OF THE WORLD." HE TRAINED "BELLE BEACH," INTO A WORLD CHAMPION... THE HIGH POINT OF HIS CAREER. THE HORSE WAS GIVEN TO TOM BY ITS OWNER AT THE AGE OF 24. MR. BASS WAS ONE OF THE GREATEST SHOW HORSE TRAINERS.

Geo Lee

MR. BASS ON BELLE BEACH

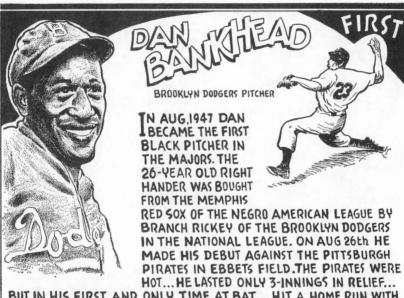

DAN BANKHEAD
FIRST

BROOKLYN DODGERS PITCHER

IN AUG,1947 DAN BECAME THE FIRST BLACK PITCHER IN THE MAJORS. THE 26-YEAR OLD RIGHT HANDER WAS BOUGHT FROM THE MEMPHIS RED SOX OF THE NEGRO AMERICAN LEAGUE BY BRANCH RICKEY OF THE BROOKLYN DODGERS IN THE NATIONAL LEAGUE. ON AUG 26th HE MADE HIS DEBUT AGAINST THE PITTSBURGH PIRATES IN EBBETS FIELD. THE PIRATES WERE HOT...HE LASTED ONLY 3-INNINGS IN RELIEF... BUT IN HIS FIRST AND ONLY TIME AT BAT... HIT A HOME RUN WITH ONE ON! A NATIVE OF BIRMINGHAM, ALA., HE BEGAN HIS CAREER AS A SHORTSTOP, WITH THE BIRMINGHAM BLACK BARONS IN 1940. A FASTBALL PITCHER, CAME TO THE MAJORS AS A STRIKE-OUT ARTIST!

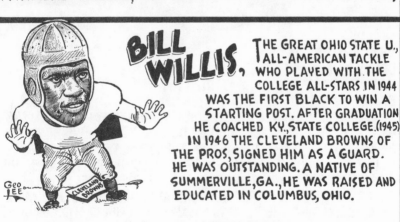

BILL WILLIS,

THE GREAT OHIO STATE U., ALL-AMERICAN TACKLE WHO PLAYED WITH THE COLLEGE ALL-STARS IN 1944 WAS THE FIRST BLACK TO WIN A STARTING POST. AFTER GRADUATION HE COACHED KY., STATE COLLEGE.(1945) IN 1946 THE CLEVELAND BROWNS OF THE PROS, SIGNED HIM AS A GUARD. HE WAS OUTSTANDING. A NATIVE OF SUMMERVILLE, GA., HE WAS RAISED AND EDUCATED IN COLUMBUS, OHIO.

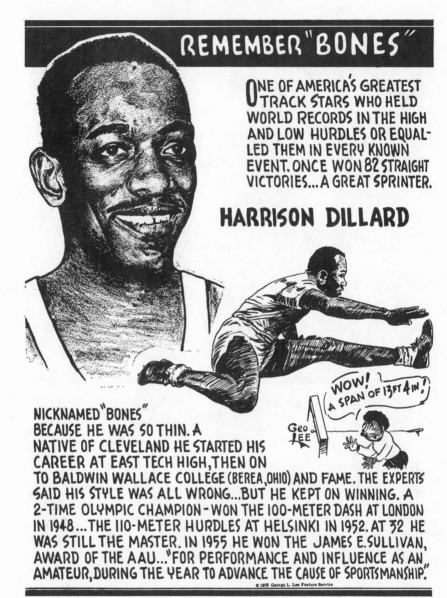

REMEMBER "BONES"

ONE OF AMERICA'S GREATEST TRACK STARS WHO HELD WORLD RECORDS IN THE HIGH AND LOW HURDLES OR EQUALLED THEM IN EVERY KNOWN EVENT. ONCE WON 82 STRAIGHT VICTORIES... A GREAT SPRINTER.

HARRISON DILLARD

WOW!
A SPAN OF 13 FT 4 IN!

Geo. LEE

NICKNAMED "BONES" BECAUSE HE WAS SO THIN. A NATIVE OF CLEVELAND HE STARTED HIS CAREER AT EAST TECH HIGH, THEN ON TO BALDWIN WALLACE COLLEGE (BEREA, OHIO) AND FAME. THE EXPERTS SAID HIS STYLE WAS ALL WRONG... BUT HE KEPT ON WINNING. A 2-TIME OLYMPIC CHAMPION - WON THE 100-METER DASH AT LONDON IN 1948... THE 110-METER HURDLES AT HELSINKI IN 1952. AT 32 HE WAS STILL THE MASTER. IN 1955 HE WON THE JAMES E. SULLIVAN, AWARD OF THE AAU..."FOR PERFORMANCE AND INFLUENCE AS AN AMATEUR, DURING THE YEAR TO ADVANCE THE CAUSE OF SPORTSMANSHIP."

© 1975 George L. Lee Feature Service

144

THE BLACK PEARL

OF THE SANTOS CLUB OF BRAZIL

THE GREATEST SOCCER PLAYER IN THE WORLD AND THE RICHEST WITH EARNINGS OF $1.5 MILLION DOLLARS A YEAR. THE SON OF A POOR PROFESSIONAL SOCCER PLAYER ON A SMALL-TIME CLUB, HE SHOWED GREAT ABILITY AT AN EARLY AGE. HE WAS THE YOUNGEST PLAYER EVER (16) CHOSEN BY THE BRAZILIAN NATIONAL TEAM. AT 17 HE LED THE TEAM TO ITS FIRST WORLD CUP CHAMPIONSHIP (1958) IN SWEDEN. PELE SCORED A WORLD RECORD OF 129 GOALS IN 1959. HE HAS BEEN NAMED MOST VALUABLE PLAYER 7 TIMES IN 12 YEARS (1970). ONCE SCORED 8 GOALS IN ONE GAME IN 1964. PELE A NATIONAL TREASURE IS BRAZIL'S GREATEST HERO. ALTHO RETIRED FROM INTERNATIONAL COMPETITION HE IS STILL ACTIVE IN SOCCER!

Geo LEE

PELE

BORN, EDSON ARANTES DE NASCIMENTO IN TRES CORACOES NEAR SANTOS, BRAZIL. WHO ROSE FROM POVERTY TO WEALTH!

PLAYING WITH SANTOS vs VASCO DE GAMA OF CARIOCA ON NOV 19, 1969, HE WAS THE FIRST PRO TO SCORE 1,000 GOALS.

© 1976 George L. Lee Feature Service

CHARLIE SIFFORD

DEAN OF THE BLACK PRO GOLFERS WAS BORN IN 1923 IN CHARLOTTE, N.C. HE BEGAN AS A CADDY AT 10. BY 15 COULD SHOOT IN THE..70's... BUT HE WANTED TO BE A BOXER... SOON HE REALIZED HE MADE A MISTAKE. HE MOVED TO PHILADELPHIA, PA., AND STARTED HIS CAREER AS A GOLFER. HE DOMINATED THE BLACK UGA NATIONALS (1953-56). HE WAS THE FIRST BLACK TO WIN A MAJOR U.S. PRO GOLF TOURNEY WHEN HE WON THE LONG BEACH TOURNEY NOV 10,'57 ($11,500). A GREAT COMPETITOR...NEARLY ALWAYS IN THE MONEY. IN 1967 HE WON THE GREATER HARTFORD OPEN ($20,000). IN 1969 THE LOS ANGELES OPEN ($20,000).

I QUIT!

SIFFORD HAS LEFT THE PGA TOUR TO BE HEAD PRO AT SLEEPY HOLLOW GOLF COURSE IN BRECKSVILLE, OHIO. (1975)

Geo Lee

PGA

HE MADE IT!

ALTHO HE PLAYED IN TOURNAMENTS SANCTIONED BY THE PGA, IT WAS NOT UNTIL NOV 1961 THAT THE PGA OPENED FULL MEMBERSHIP TO BLACKS...CHARLIE HAD MADE HIS EFFORTS PAY OFF.....

© 1975 George L. Lee Feature Service

TENNIS $ $ $ $ $ ANYONE

A SUPER-STAR IN TENNIS WHO HAS OPENED THE DOOR FOR ASPIRING BLACK YOUTHS IN THE WORLD OF TENNIS.

ARTHUR ASHE

OF RICHMOND, VA., STARTED HIS CAREER AT THE AGE OF 7.

GEO LEE

TODAY AT 31 HE IS PRES., OF THE ASSOCIATION OF TENNIS PROFESSIONALS. AFTER A GREAT CAREER...SOMETIMES LOSING THE BIG ONES...HE HAS REACHED THE TOP. IN MAY (1975) HE WON THE WORLD CHAMPIONSHIP TENNIS TITLE IN DALLAS, TEX. LAST YEAR HE EARNED $150,000...FIRST 6-MONTHS OF 1975 HE HAS SURPASSED THAT FIGURE ...$177,000! ARTHUR HAS COME A LONG WAY DESPITE THE OBSTACLES. AT 10 HE WAS DENIED THE RIGHT TO PLAY IN A PUBLIC PARK CITY TOURNAMENT...BECAUSE HE WAS BLACK.

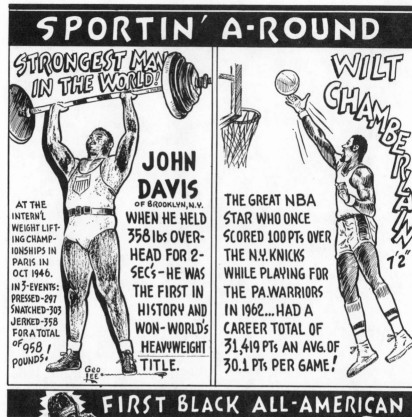

SPORTIN' A-ROUND

STRONGEST MAN IN THE WORLD!

JOHN DAVIS
OF BROOKLYN, N.Y.

AT THE INTERN'L WEIGHT LIFTING CHAMPIONSHIPS IN PARIS IN OCT 1946. IN 3-EVENTS: PRESSED-297 SNATCHED-303 JERKED-358 FOR A TOTAL OF 958 POUNDS!

WHEN HE HELD 358 lbs OVERHEAD FOR 2-SEC's — HE WAS THE FIRST IN HISTORY AND WON—WORLD's HEAVYWEIGHT TITLE.

Geo Lee

WILT CHAMBERLAIN 7'2"

THE GREAT NBA STAR WHO ONCE SCORED 100 PTs OVER THE N.Y. KNICKS WHILE PLAYING FOR THE PA. WARRIORS IN 1962...HAD A CAREER TOTAL OF 31,419 PTs AN AVG. OF 30.1 PTs PER GAME!

FIRST BLACK ALL-AMERICAN

FRITZ POLLARD

A FOOTBALL LEGEND WHO STARRED WITH BROWN UNIV. (1915-16) WHEN THEY BEAT YALE AND HARVARD WAS NAMED TO WALTER CAMP'S FIRST ALL-AMERICAN TEAM (1916).

HE PLAYED IN THE FIRST ROSE BOWL GAME JAN 1, 1916 WITH BROWN U. vs WASH. STATE.

© 1976 George L. Lee Feature Service

EDDIE TOLAN

ONE OF TRACKS IMMORTALS. HE CAME OUT OF CASS HI-SCHOOL, DETROIT AND THE U OF MICHIGAN TO TAKE TOP HONORS IN THE DASHES. BORN IN DENVER, COLO., THE 5'4" SPEEDSTER WHO SET A WORLD'S RECORD FOR THE 100-YD DASH (9.5 SEC) IN 1929 WAS BIG TEN CHAMP ALSO IN THE 220-YD DASH (1930-31). A 1931 GRADUATE OF THE

U OF MICHIGAN, HE WAS A STAR OF THE 1932 OLYMPICS IN LOS ANGELES. TOLAN WON 3 GOLD MEDALS AND THE FIRST BLACK TO WIN THE 100-METER DASH AND SET A WORLD'S RECORD OF

GEO LEE

LAST AT THE START METCALFE CAUGHT EDDIE AT 90-METERS BUT EDDIE BEAT HIM TO THE FINISH!

10.3. IN THE 200-METER HE SET AN OLYMPIC RECORD OF 21.2...HE RAN ANCHOR ON THE WINNING U.S. RELAY TEAM. EDDIE WAS THE SECOND BLACK TO ENTER THE MICHIGAN SPORTS HALL OF FAME IN 1958. JOE LOUIS THE FIRST. THE GREAT LITTLE SPRINTER DIED 1967.

© 1976 George L. Lee Feature Service

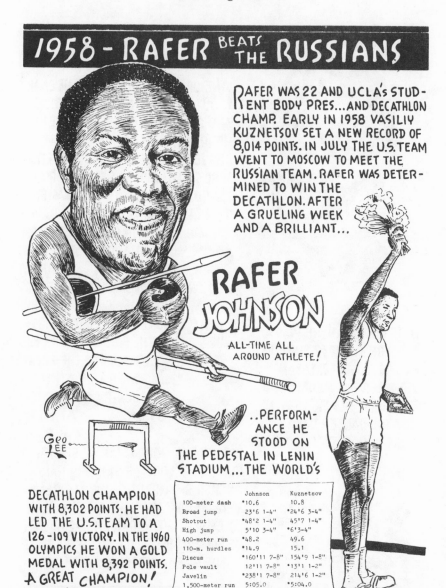

1958 - RAFER BEATS THE RUSSIANS

RAFER WAS 22 AND UCLA's STUD-ENT BODY PRES...AND DECATHLON CHAMP. EARLY IN 1958 VASILIY KUZNETSOV SET A NEW RECORD OF 8,014 POINTS. IN JULY THE U.S. TEAM WENT TO MOSCOW TO MEET THE RUSSIAN TEAM. RAFER WAS DETER-MINED TO WIN THE DECATHLON. AFTER A GRUELING WEEK AND A BRILLIANT...

RAFER JOHNSON

ALL-TIME ALL AROUND ATHLETE!

..PERFORM-ANCE HE STOOD ON THE PEDESTAL IN LENIN STADIUM...THE WORLD'S

Geo Lee

DECATHLON CHAMPION WITH 8,302 POINTS. HE HAD LED THE U.S. TEAM TO A 126-109 VICTORY. IN THE 1960 OLYMPICS HE WON A GOLD MEDAL WITH 8,392 POINTS. A GREAT CHAMPION!

© 1976 George L. Lee Feature Service

	Johnson	Kuznetsov
100-meter dash	*10.6	10.8
Broad jump	23'6 1-4"	*24'6 3-4"
Shotput	*48'2 1-4"	45'7 1-4"
High jump	5'10 3-4"	*6'3-4"
400-meter run	*48.2	49.6
110-m. hurdles	*14.9	15.1
Discus	*160'11 7-8"	154'9 1-8"
Pole vault	12'11 7-8"	*13'1 1-2"
Javelin	*238'1 7-8"	214'6 1-2"
1,500-meter run	5:05.0	*5:04.0

1960 — OLYMPIC GOLD

RAFER JOHNSON

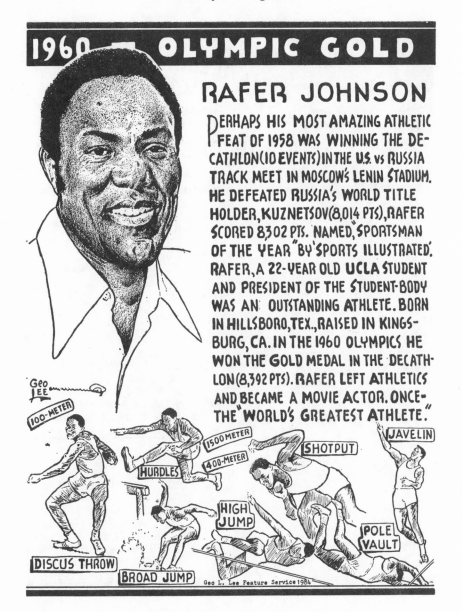

PERHAPS HIS MOST AMAZING ATHLETIC FEAT OF 1958 WAS WINNING THE DECATHLON (10 EVENTS) IN THE U.S. vs RUSSIA TRACK MEET IN MOSCOW'S LENIN STADIUM. HE DEFEATED RUSSIA'S WORLD TITLE HOLDER, KUZNETSOV (8,014 PTS), RAFER SCORED 8,302 PTS. NAMED "SPORTSMAN OF THE YEAR" BY 'SPORTS ILLUSTRATED'. RAFER, A 22-YEAR OLD **UCLA** STUDENT AND PRESIDENT OF THE STUDENT-BODY WAS AN OUTSTANDING ATHLETE. BORN IN HILLSBORO, TEX., RAISED IN KINGSBURG, CA. IN THE 1960 OLYMPICS HE WON THE GOLD MEDAL IN THE DECATHLON (8,392 PTS). RAFER LEFT ATHLETICS AND BECAME A MOVIE ACTOR. ONCE-THE "WORLD'S GREATEST ATHLETE."

Geo Lee

100-METER

1500 METER

400-METER

HURDLES

SHOTPUT

JAVELIN

HIGH JUMP

POLE VAULT

DISCUS THROW

BROAD JUMP

Geo L. Lee Feature Service 1984

ALL-AMERICAN
COLLEGE PRESIDENT
U.S. AMBASSADOR
BUSINESS DIRECTOR

JEROME (BRUD) HOLLAND

A NATIVE OF AUBURN, N.Y.

1. RECEIVED HIS B.A. FROM CORNELL AND PH.D FROM THE U. OF PENNSYLVANIA, IN SOCIOLOGY. AN ALL-AMERICAN END AT CORNELL IN 1938-39. TAUGHT AT LINCOLN U. AND TENN. A+I. UNIV. IN 1953 HE BECAME PRESIDENT OF

2. DELAWARE STATE COLLEGE AND NAMED 9th PRESIDENT OF HAMPTON INSTITUTE (VA)., IN 1960. SERVED AS A MEMBER OF THE STATE DEPT'S LIAISON COMMITTEE.

3. NAMED BY PRES. NIXON IN 1970 TO THE POST OF U.S. ENVOY TO SWEDEN. AMBASSADOR HOLLAND SERVED WITH DIGNITY UNDER DIFFICULT CONDITIONS DUE TO SWEDEN'S ANTI-WAR POSITION IN VIETNAM. IN 1972 HE WAS APPOINTED AS THE FIRST BLACK

4. DIRECTOR OF THE N.Y. STOCK EXCHANGE IN ITS 180-YEAR HISTORY. ALSO A BOARD MEMBER ON OTHER FIRMS, INCLUDING AT&T AND UNION CARBIDE CORP. HE RECEIVED THE NAT'L CONFERENCE OF CHRISTIANS AND JEWS' 8th CHARLES EVANS HUGHES AWARD (1972) - FOR COURAGEOUS LEADERSHIP!

© 1975 George L. Lee Feature Service

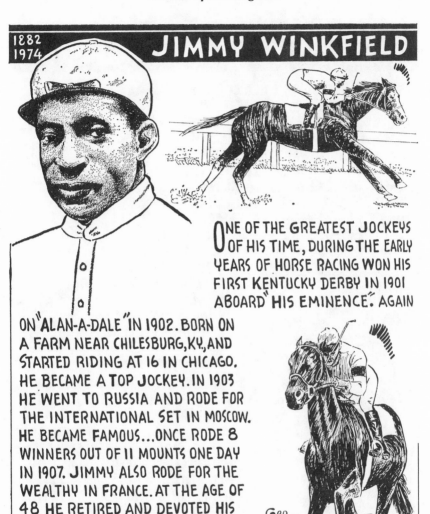

1882 1974

JIMMY WINKFIELD

ONE OF THE GREATEST JOCKEYS OF HIS TIME, DURING THE EARLY YEARS OF HORSE RACING WON HIS FIRST KENTUCKY DERBY IN 1901 ABOARD "HIS EMINENCE". AGAIN ON "ALAN-A-DALE" IN 1902. BORN ON A FARM NEAR CHILESBURG, KY., AND STARTED RIDING AT 16 IN CHICAGO. HE BECAME A TOP JOCKEY. IN 1903 HE WENT TO RUSSIA AND RODE FOR THE INTERNATIONAL SET IN MOSCOW. HE BECAME FAMOUS...ONCE RODE 8 WINNERS OUT OF 11 MOUNTS ONE DAY IN 1907. JIMMY ALSO RODE FOR THE WEALTHY IN FRANCE. AT THE AGE OF 48 HE RETIRED AND DEVOTED HIS LIFE TO TRAINING AND RACING HIS OWN HORSES. HE DIED IN PARIS AT THE AGE OF 92... A GREAT HORSEMAN!

Geo. LEE

SPORTIN' AROUND...

ENTERED BASEBALL'S HALL OF FAME ON AUG 8,1977... A VERY INTERESTING CAREER. BORN IN DALLAS, TEX., ON JAN 31, 1931. HE NEVER PLAYED BASEBALL IN HIGH SCHOOL. HE WAS DISCOVERED PLAYING SOFTBALL. HE JUMPED FROM A NEGRO LEAGUE TO THE CUBS(1953-71). KNOWN AS "MR CUB"... HE NEVER PLAYED IN THE MINORS. ERNIE HAD A GREAT CAREER: 512 HOMERS-OVER 40 IN-A-SEASON 5 TIMES-5 GRAND SLAMS IN 1955-MOST VALUABLE PLAYER 1958-59...

ERNIE BANKS
SHORTSTOP
CHICAGO
CUBS

FIRST SHORTSTOP TO HIT 47 HR's IN 1958-BEST FIELDING SS-AVERAGE .985 WITH ONLY 12 ERRORS IN 1959.

Geo LEE

ERNIE DAVIS

1940
1963

HALFBACK, SYRACUSE U., (N Y). STEPPED INTO THE POSITION OF THE GREAT JIM BROWN AND WORE HIS No. 44...THEN WENT ON TO BEAT JIM'S COLLEGE RECORDS! ERNIE'S GREAT COLLEGE CAREER REACHED THE HEIGHTS WHEN HE WAS NAMED AS THE BEST COLLEGE "PLAYER OF THE YEAR"(1961) ...AND AWARDED THE "HEISMAN TROPHY." THE FIRST BLACK TO WIN THE PRESTIGIOUS AWARD IN ITS 27-YEAR HISTORY. HE FOLLOWED JIM TO THE PROS...BUT FATE THREW HIM FOR A LOSS! HE WAS DOWNED BY "LEUKEMIA" AT AGE 23.

1985 GEO L. LEE FEATURE SERVICE

SPORTING AROUND!

JESSE OWENS

SET 3 NEW WORLD'S RECORDS AND EQUALLED ANOTHER IN ONE DAY!

WOW! 26'8¼" WHATTA JUMP

A MEMBER OF THE OHIO STATE U. TRACK TEAM HAD A RECORD DAY - ON MAY 25, 1935 AT ANN HARBOR, MICH., HE SET 3 NEW WORLD RECORDS - 220 YD-DASH IN 20.3; 220 YD-LOW HURDLES IN 22.6; BROAD JUMPED 26'8¼" AND EQUALLED THE 100 YD-DASH IN 9.4.

GEO LEE

MARSHALL W. "MAJOR" TAYLOR
1878 - 1932

"KING OF THE CYCLISTS"

HE WON THE WORLD CYCLE RACING CHAMPIONSHIP IN 1899 AND THE U.S. TITLE IN 1900. IN 1901 HE WENT TO EUROPE AND MET ALL-COMERS AND DEFEATED THEM. "THE FASTEST BIKE RIDER IN THE WORLD."

JACKIE ROBINSON

FIRST BLACK IN MAJOR LEAGUE BASEBALL - STARRED IN 4 MAJOR SPORTS IN COLLEGE. FOOTBALL, BASKETBALL, TRACK AND BASEBALL FOR 6-YEARS FOR A TOTAL OF 24 LETTERS.

BUDDY YOUNG

PLAYING HIS FRESHMAN YEAR AT THE U. OF ILLINOIS IN 1944, EQUALLED THE 20-YEAR RECORD OF THE FAMED RED GRANGE BY SCORING 13 TOUCHDOWNS!

Chicago Defender   February 2, 1935

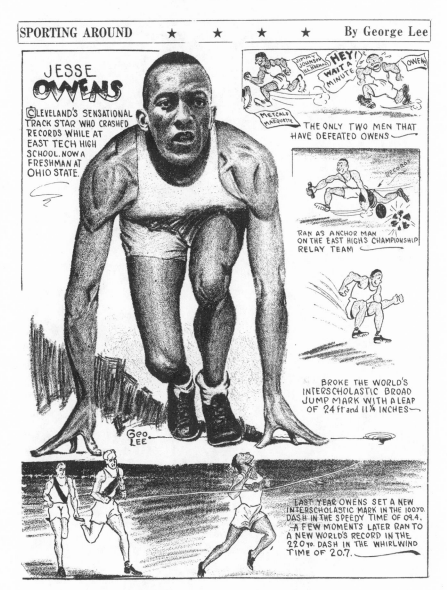

Chicago Defender   February 3, 1934

Pittsburgh Courier   September 4, 1937

June 1934

159

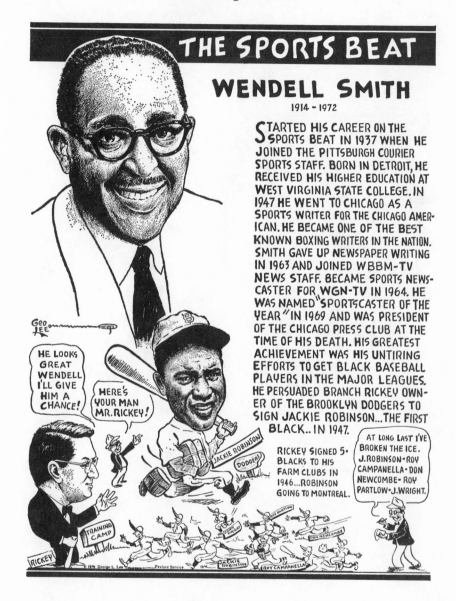

THE SPORTS BEAT

WENDELL SMITH
1914 - 1972

STARTED HIS CAREER ON THE SPORTS BEAT IN 1937 WHEN HE JOINED THE PITTSBURGH COURIER SPORTS STAFF. BORN IN DETROIT, HE RECEIVED HIS HIGHER EDUCATION AT WEST VIRGINIA STATE COLLEGE. IN 1947 HE WENT TO CHICAGO AS A SPORTS WRITER FOR THE CHICAGO AMER-ICAN. HE BECAME ONE OF THE BEST KNOWN BOXING WRITERS IN THE NATION. SMITH GAVE UP NEWSPAPER WRITING IN 1963 AND JOINED WBBM-TV NEWS STAFF. BECAME SPORTS NEWS-CASTER FOR WGN-TV IN 1964. HE WAS NAMED "SPORTSCASTER OF THE YEAR" IN 1969 AND WAS PRESIDENT OF THE CHICAGO PRESS CLUB AT THE TIME OF HIS DEATH. HIS GREATEST ACHIEVEMENT WAS HIS UNTIRING EFFORTS TO GET BLACK BASEBALL PLAYERS IN THE MAJOR LEAGUES. HE PERSUADED BRANCH RICKEY OWN-ER OF THE BROOKLYN DODGERS TO SIGN JACKIE ROBINSON...THE FIRST BLACK.. IN 1947.

Geo Lee

HE LOOKS GREAT WENDELL I'LL GIVE HIM A CHANCE!

HERE'S YOUR MAN MR. RICKEY!

JACKIE ROBINSON

DODGERS

RICKEY SIGNED 5 BLACKS TO HIS FARM CLUBS IN 1946...ROBINSON GOING TO MONTREAL.

AT LONG LAST I'VE BROKEN THE ICE. J.ROBINSON-ROY CAMPANELLA-DON NEWCOMBE-ROY PARTLOW-J.WRIGHT.

TRAINING CAMP

RICKEY

© 1974 George L. Lee — Feature Service

JACKIE ROBINSON

ROY CAMPANELLA

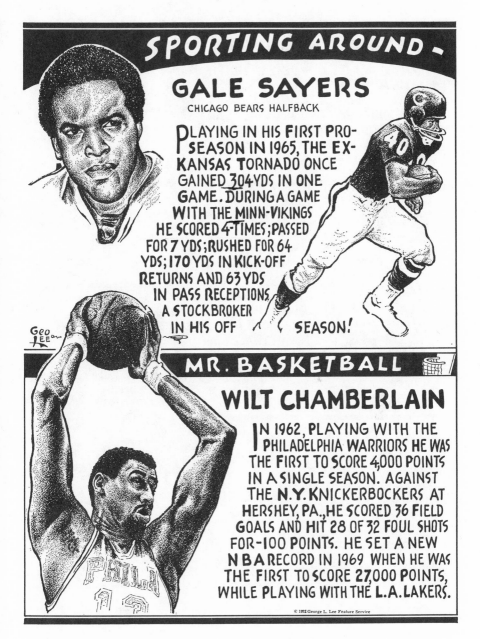

SPORTING AROUND -

GALE SAYERS
CHICAGO BEARS HALFBACK

PLAYING IN HIS FIRST PRO-SEASON IN 1965, THE EX-KANSAS TORNADO ONCE GAINED 304 YDS IN ONE GAME. DURING A GAME WITH THE MINN-VIKINGS HE SCORED 4 TIMES; PASSED FOR 7 YDS; RUSHED FOR 64 YDS; 170 YDS IN KICK-OFF RETURNS AND 63 YDS IN PASS RECEPTIONS. A STOCKBROKER IN HIS OFF SEASON!

MR. BASKETBALL

WILT CHAMBERLAIN

IN 1962, PLAYING WITH THE PHILADELPHIA WARRIORS HE WAS THE FIRST TO SCORE 4,000 POINTS IN A SINGLE SEASON. AGAINST THE N.Y. KNICKERBOCKERS AT HERSHEY, PA., HE SCORED 36 FIELD GOALS AND HIT 28 OF 32 FOUL SHOTS FOR-100 POINTS. HE SET A NEW NBA RECORD IN 1969 WHEN HE WAS THE FIRST TO SCORE 27,000 POINTS, WHILE PLAYING WITH THE L.A. LAKERS.

FRAZIER THOMPSON

First Black to compete in Notre Dame athletics. A crack sprinter he was the first Black to win a Notre Dame Monogram (1945-46). An honor student from Philadelphia he entered in July 1944. A Navy V-12 pre- medic student.

ARTHUR WILSON

A Navy V-12 student was the first Black athlete to play on a Princeton Univ., varsity team. A basketball star he was the first to receive a letter (1945-46).

ALICE COACHMAN

The only woman of the 1948 U.S. Olympic squad to win a gold medal in track and field in the high jump. A sprinter and star high jumper of the women's track team of Tuskegee Institute - won 3 championships on the 1945 Nat'l A.A.U. Women's All-America track team.

© 1973 George L. Lee Feature Service

Index

Index

Index